MORE
like HIM

God Bless you
as you follow
Him more closely.
Jim Littles
Luke 6:40

MORE
like HIM

THE PROCESS OF
SPIRITUAL FORMATION

JAMES A. LITTLES JR.

WORD AFLAME PRESS
WELDON SPRING, MO

Word Aflame Press
36 Research Park Court
Weldon Spring, MO 63304
pentecostalpublishing.com

All Scripture verses quoted are from the King James Version.

Cover design by Elizabeth Loyd

Printed in the United States of America

28 27 26 25 24 23 22 21 20 19   1 2 3 4 5

Library of Congress Cataloging-in-Publication Data

Names: Littles, James A., Jr., 1961- author.
Title: More like him : the process of spiritual formation / by James
     A. Littles, Jr.
Description: Weldon Spring : Word Aflame Press, 2019.
Identifiers: LCCN 2019011080 (print) | ISBN 9780757760891
Subjects: LCSH: Spiritual formation.
Classification: LCC BV4511 .L575 2019 (print) | LCC BV4511
     (ebook) | DDC 248.4--dc23
LC record available at https://lccn.loc.gov/2019011080
LC ebook record available at https://lccn.loc.gov/2019980457

I am honored to dedicate this book to my parents, Rev. James A. Littles Sr. and Eva R. Littles. They provided the seedbed for my spiritual formation through their lifelong commitment to making disciples in Illinois, New York, and Missouri. I learned more from walking with them than I have from any other form of study.

Contents

Preface

Readers peruse books for a wide variety of reasons. I have a few technical books on vintage fountain pen repair that I consult when a new find presents a challenge I have not encountered before. Some of my books inform, entertain, distract, provide perspective, or prepare for a pending trip to a new culture. Of course theological dictionaries, encyclopedias, and commentaries play an important role in my library as well.

This book seeks to play a different role. It seeks to transform disciples as they read, reflect, pray, practice, repent, learn, and grow. I hope to join the readers as an author on the journey myself rather than as a credentialed expert that sets me apart. If the readers let me journey and mature with them, then I have the authority to write the book.

I have had the privilege to travel with several groups of disciples during my lifetime. Years in an upstate New York church planters' home provided the early seedbed for my formation. I am thankful for churches in Dover, Delaware; Florissant, Missouri; and Garland, Texas, for twenty-eight years of the journey. Years spent teaching and learning with students at Kent Christian College, Gateway College of Evangelism, Urshan Graduate School of Theology, and Urshan College offered many opportunities to wrestle with the call to spiritual formation on a consistent basis. I am deeply indebted to those students and colleagues who shared their lives with me during those years.

Since no one can be an expert in spiritual formation, I do not write this book expecting everyone to agree on every point. We all still look through "a glass darkly." Someday we shall see Christ face-to-face—at that point the book will have no value beyond seeing our feeble attempts to respond to God's grace and mission and seeing God's mercy in working with and through His church during our journey. I also look forward to reading the works of other brothers and sisters on the journey to being and serving like Christ.

Every type of book comes with its own reading guidelines. One does not usually read a technical manual like a science fiction book. A book on spiritual formation must start with an open and honest dependence on God's grace. Without God's sustaining grace we will not be able to face areas needing change, have courage to take the necessary steps under the prayerful eye of others, or be able to sustain our steps until we have experienced significant spiritual transformation. Prayer for God to be glorified with our lives comes next. Anything that brings us glory *de*forms us rather than makes us more like the Master. Another component of the journey is to recognize our defensiveness and efforts to seek pain reduction as our primary goal. Spiritual formation does not seek the same goals as psychotherapeutic closure. Being transformed will reveal areas of spiritual immaturity and brokenness. God's grace gives us confidence in those moments that our Teacher values us as His own and will be with us as we are renewed in His image.

Most of us stopped reading books in groups once we got out of elementary school. Spiritual formation books work best in community because we must be formed as Christ's body rather than free-standing individuals that have everything together. Take time with others to discuss the Spirit's claims on your life.

Finally, be willing to limit your areas of growth to one or two spiritual dimensions at a time. As the Spirit reveals areas needing renewed transformational focus, pursue that area until the process begins to produce fruit. While you may want to read through the whole book over a given period of time, you will need to focus on one chapter at a time to move from informational to transformational reading.

Thank you for letting me walk with you on this exciting journey of spiritual formation. I look forward to seeing Jesus' image and mission more fully formed in us.

Let us pray.

Lord, we give You thanks for inviting us to participate in Your image and mission. Give us the courage to receive wave after wave of grace as we become the people You called us to be even before the foundation of the world.

In Jesus' name,
Amen

1 | *Walking in Newness of Life*

I remember the day my father/pastor baptized me in our small congregation in Galatia, Illinois. The year was 1967. I would turn six years old the next week. Part of our humanity rests in the ability to remember and make meaning in our lives. Most Christians can tell stories of their conversion experience. Some may have dramatic stories of changing direction in moments of crises, while others experienced a less dramatic transition while being part of a family that valued faith.

Memories of my baptism from fifty years ago still bring thoughts of water bubbles, smiles on my parents' faces, being welcomed by our church family, and trees that seemed much greener than when I went into church that day. I had committed to God all of the wickedness in my life. I do not think the accumulated sins contained too many items in those days, yet those sins still needed the work of redemption. While much water has gone under the bridge, and some has swelled over the bridge as well, I still quest for a deeper relationship with Christ a half century later.

As a child I could tell my Sunday school teacher and my pastor the right number of keys in the plan of salvation. Certainly I was not the only child to make a key ring that held mighty terms of repentance, baptism in Jesus' name, and the Holy Spirit (of course I would have said Holy Ghost in 1967). With new birth we all joined a very large and very old family—a family that grows daily as it lives out God's missionary purposes in the world. That birth, however, serves as a wonderful beginning rather than an end goal.

Scripture gives us powerful witness to God's assurance that our lives together culminate in accordance with "the good pleasure of his will" (Ephesians 1:5). In fact, Paul went on to say, "That in the dispensation of the fulness of times he might gather together in one all things in Christ, both which are in heaven, and which are on earth; even in him; in whom also we have obtained an inheritance, being predestinated according to the purpose of him who worketh all things after the counsel of his own will" (Ephesians 1:10–11).

God has already brought these promises to pass through His will, predestining power, and loving grace. While some folks see predestination of the whole body and others see predestination on a more individual level, all must agree that God's will shall be done through Christ.

On the other hand, Scripture also speaks of a fear that some will not enter that rest. "Let us therefore fear, lest, a promise being left us of entering into his rest, any of you should seem to come short of it. For unto us was the gospel preached, as well as unto them: but the word preached did not profit them, not being mixed with faith in them that heard it" (Hebrews 4:1–2).

God has given abundant promises and grace to ensure "whosoever will" shall be saved, yet we face the paradox of laboring to enter into that rest (Hebrews 4:11).

Personal Reflection

Briefly write out your conversion story. Tell the story as if you are explaining it to someone who has no idea about what it means to follow Jesus. Include influences that called you to faith, steps along the way in your conversion, and challenges you faced along the way. Witness to your personal experience rather than fitting a prescribed narrative.

THE WAY OF SPIRITUAL FORMATION

All disciples, and the communities they share, have the wonderful opportunity to put away immature faith as they seek to live out their new identity. While key rings help children think about going through the open door of relationship with Christ, that cardboard Sunday school class project will not be sufficient as God calls them to spiritual maturity. In fact they must mature beyond this foundational truth if they hope to teach others.[1]

Perhaps an example from grade school would help to illustrate the point. When I taught second grade math, I told students the big number always had to go on the top when they subtracted numbers. I did not tell the whole truth; maybe I was not telling the truth at all. As students learned the basic concept of subtraction, they needed to grasp the meaning of taking away numbers. The big number had to go on top. Using food examples always helped in the exercise. If you have six candy bars and your friends eat two of them, then how many candy bars do you have left? The big number goes on top . . . always (for now). Second graders needed to understand subtraction before they were ready for negative numbers. Of course some of them could go on to irrational numbers, imaginary numbers, and the world where mathematicians seem to rarely even use numbers at all. Just as a math teacher carefully leads students to more complex and important mathematical principles, our Teacher carefully leads us to more faithfully follow His example.

The way of discipleship calls us individually and corporately to continually become more like Jesus, our Teacher. Fortunately our Teacher provides simple starting places. Ongoing maturity continues to bless us with endless transformational opportunities. *Spiritual formation is the lifelong personal and communal commitment to know Christ, to be remade in His image as a part of new creation, and to be on His mission*. We start with new birth and adoption, but we must continue to grow if we wish to fulfill our Teacher's good pleasure.

Followers of Christ will have to go beyond society's understanding of spirituality. One research project from Bowling Green State University defined spirituality as a search for the sacred.[2] Christians must go further than this popular understanding of spirituality. They will pursue both loving God and loving their neighbors as themselves (Matthew 22:37–40). This new life of love, a life made possible by Jesus' death and resurrection, reorients people from separation from God and His creation to lives which bring God glory (Ephesians 1:14).

The term *spiritual formation* emphasizes the process of maturing in faith.[3] While some will use the term *spiritual discipline* to focus on the practices, spiritual formation focuses on the goal of being formed in Christ. This book invites us to participate in God's re-creative work by joining with Him in all areas of life. For example, our prayer life undergoes transformation as we mature in Christ. This perspective on prayer calls us to mature in the content, process, and expected outcomes of prayer. Of course, if we are not praying, then starting to pray will be a part of this perspective as well.

Spiritual formation centers on the person and work of Christ. "God so loved the world, that he gave his only begotten Son" (John 3:16). He did so to achieve His divine purpose of reconciling the whole world unto Himself. Consequently we have the wonder of being God's ambassadors in the world, ambassadors with both the deeds and words of reconciliation.[4] Our new nature springs from being reconciled to God and makes us the very righteousness of God.

Spiritual formation calls us to see salvation and spiritual disciplines as more than a means of escape.[5] The *sacred escape* paradigm sees following Jesus as a kind of Pied Piper who leads us out of our messy world and difficult situations. Sacred escapism tends to look away from Jesus' incarnational identity. Jesus came as fully God and fully human. Biblical writers witnessed how they had heard Jesus, seen Jesus, and handled Jesus (I John 1:1). This Jesus wanted to send His followers into the world just as the Father had sent Him. Because His own work would be lived out in His disciples, He prayed for them. "I pray not that thou shouldest take them out of the world, but that thou shouldest keep them from the evil" (John 17:15). Spiritual formation will send us into the world to continue Jesus' mission rather than merely seeking to keep us separated from the world. Jesus' disciples must pursue incarnational rather than excarnational living. Separation from the world prepares us to go back into the world. While some spiritual formation may attend to getting the world out of disciples, those same spiritual formation practices will send us right back into the world as Christ's ambassadors. Disciples can do nothing else. They must follow Jesus.

Personal Reflection

   Review your spiritual formation from the last month.
   1. *What did you pray about? What biblical passages did you read? What other spiritual activities did you practice to become more like Christ?*

   2. *Discuss your answers in number 1 with a spiritual friend. Carefully examine the degree to which your answers focus on:*
        a. *becoming more like Christ*
        b. *practicing behaviors out of obligation*
        c. *seeking to be ready for Heaven*
        d. *preparing to better serve in the world*

   3. *How might you pray, read your Bible, or do other spiritual activities differently with a focus on following Jesus' mission in the world?*

ON HOLINESS AND COMMUNITY

Modern Pentecostalism began as a part of the Holiness movement in the twentieth century. Apostolic Pentecostals continue to celebrate their holiness identity in the twenty-first century. Readers of I Peter 1 marvel at the invitation to demonstrate holiness in all areas of life. The blood of Christ makes holiness a possibility for His followers. While we cannot earn holiness through gold or our own efforts, we can joyfully "obey the truth through the Spirit unto unfeigned love of the brethren" (I Peter 1.22).

Spiritual formation intentionally embraces the wonder of holiness. This holiness does not earn status with God, get His attention, or buy a spot on the "glory train" that takes ticket holders through Heaven's portals. *Excarnational* holiness keeps working on getting sin out of Jesus' followers. On the other hand, *incarnational* holiness joyfully responds to the invitation to God's holiness, sending them back into the world as servants of God. They pursue holiness in their inner being, finances, leisure, corporate relationships, family, and other areas of life. They celebrate the opportunity to be more like Christ as they serve on His mission.

Fortunately the call to holiness, like salvation, comes in the context of Christ's body, the church. A holiness people mature in their calling to be a "chosen generation, a royal priesthood, an holy nation, a peculiar people; that [they] should shew forth the praises of him who hath called [them] out of darkness into his marvellous light" (I Peter 2:9). Holy communities support each other as they mature in Christ and serve the world together. Their hope rests in the One who calls, equips, and sends them to be salt, light, and a city on a hill.[6] Holy communities do not succumb to excarnational minimum standards, nor do they live anxiously wondering if they can ever measure up to their holy God. Rather than trying to earn their own salvation, they freely receive His holiness and follow His leading to live holy. They become holy as He is holy.

Personal Reflection

Consider a holiness question a new convert may face. How could you help the new convert reframe that question in terms of being like Christ and being a living witness in the world?

SPIRITUAL GIFTING ON THE MISSION

Spiritual formation begs for a renewed focus on the work of the Holy Spirit. Pentecostals and the wider evangelical community use the term "born again" or "new birth" to encapsulate the wonder of transformation that happens at conversion. Jesus used this language of being born again (or born from above) in His late night conversation with Nicodemus in John 3. The radical change from the kingdom of sin to Jesus' new kingdom certainly does reflect a new beginning for His followers. In fact Paul expressed the wonder of new creatureliness to be a total transformation, "If any man be in Christ, he is a new creature: old things are passed away; behold, all things are become new" (II Corinthians 5:17). This new creature identity comes through baptism in water and Spirit.

New birth, however, is not the only New Testament image to convey our new identity in Christ's family. For spiritual formation purposes, disciples need to understand the role of adoption as seen in Romans 8:15, Galatians 4:5, and Ephesians 1:5. Adoption in the Roman and Jewish world served different purposes than it does in the contemporary Western world. Adoption served to ensure the continuation of a person's lineage, business, or empire. Jacob's decision to adopt Joseph's two sons, Manasseh and Ephraim, elevated them to full-son status as inheritors. Roman emperors, such as Julius Caesar, used adoption to solidify their legacy and secure the empire in critical times of transition. This adoption brought grown men with a proven leadership record into an emperor-in-waiting status.

Adopted sons and daughters receive full rights and responsibilities with natural born children. Once the judge terminated the former father's rights, the former father had no claim on his adult children. While new birth shows the beginning (that is an infant spiritual relationship with the family of God), adoption speaks to the Kingdom potential in God's new sons and daughters. Even in the first days of new life, all men and women should recognize their right to call, "Abba, Father," rather than surrendering to the "spirit of bondage again to fear" (Romans 8:15). We should not, however, see this as merely being released from fear to joyful service. Once the Holy Spirit takes up residence in people's lives, they must realize God chose them with a purpose. They would continue Jesus' ministry and do even greater works than their Teacher (John 14:12). All four Gospels end with Jesus sending His small group of followers to continue His mission. Of course Jesus still sends us today.

Spiritual formation for adopted sons and daughters must address this shift in life's purposes. While new birth extends the opportunity to live in the Kingdom, adoption speaks to the need to identify, develop, and use spiritual gifts for Kingdom purposes. Jesus' Kingdom parables included distribution of resources to stewards as a way to address this related concept of being chosen with purpose. (See Matthew 25:14–30.)

Personal Reflection

While we all celebrate the wonder of new birth, we must also see our adoption through the lens of purposeful identity transformation. Read Jesus' commission at the end of each Gospel. How has God gifted you to be part of that mission in the world?

CONCLUSION

As we progress through this extended look at spiritual formation, we should feel both the centripetal and centrifugal forces of the Spirit. The centripetal force draws us ever closer to the center of God as we are renewed day-by-day in the image of Christ. On the other hand the Spirit's centrifugal force sends us out into the world. This centrifugal force goes from "Jerusalem, and in all Judea, and in Samaria, and unto the uttermost part of the earth" (Acts 1:8). The Spirit's dynamic power always sends the people of God with gifts. They go in the comfort of the Spirit with words to share. They go with spiritual authority and gifting. They go as one body with differing gifts—gifts graciously bestowed by God.[7] Growing in these gifts requires spiritual formation. Spiritual formation ensures that saints are not "conformed to this world: but [are] transformed by the renewing of [their] mind that [they] may prove that good, and acceptable, and perfect will of God" (Romans 12:2).

New Testament leadership functions in close relationship with the gifting of God's people. Paul provides one list of church leadership roles in Ephesians 4. Leadership gifts to the church serve to equip the saints for their work of ministry. Spiritual formation requires developing spiritual gifts in a community of believers. In this case the New Testament illustrates a major transition from the Spirit's work in the Old Testament. Prior to Acts 2 the Spirit seemed to operate in only a few people such as the tabernacle engineer, judges, prophets, generals, and kings. In the New Testament, however, this Spirit came upon all who were gathered in the upper room. Peter proclaimed the fulfillment of Joel's prophecy where young and old, male and female alike would operate under the Spirit's leading.[8] Throughout this book spiritual formation explores the quest to be like Christ on the individual level and live out the gifts in the community of saints.

Spiritual gifting plays a significant role in how the church fulfills God's purposes. An example can be seen in God's conference with Abraham before the destruction of Sodom and Gomorrah (Genesis 18:17–23). God sets the stage for the conversation by asking whether or not He can hide His pending intervention in Sodom and Gomorrah given the promises He had already made to Abraham. God's call to Abraham and Sarah included the promise to bless all the nations of the earth through them. Now God considered destroying two cities in His chosen couple's proximity. In addition to this nation-blessing responsibility, Abraham would teach his children and household to do justice and judgment. When God stated that His intention was to see if the cities actually lived in accordance with their reputation, the text points to a differing response between the angels and Abraham. The angels knew sin could not coexist with holiness, so they went toward the cities. Abraham, on the other hand, drew near to God for deeper conversation. Abraham's intercession came out of his particular spiritual gifting—justice and judgment. God had given him the gift of justice, so his prayer addressed justice issues.

While disciples will seek to love the world in Christ's name, they will do so in relationship with their giftings. Paul's gift list in Romans 12 reminds us of the role of grace and faith in living in relationship with other members of the body. God distributes spiritual gifts such as prophecy and showing mercy by grace. Saints live out their gifts in accordance with the measure of faith in their lives. Spiritual formation intentionally examines ways in which disciples can grow in their gifts. Members of Christ's body will contribute in different ways. In fact one primary reason disciples gather together is to "consider one another to provoke unto love and to good works" (Hebrews 10:24). Gathered times of worship and fellowship should provide space and intentional efforts in developing the capacity for and faithfulness to these spiritual gifts.

Personal Reflection

What gifts has God placed in your life? How do these gifts combine with the gifts of other people in your local congregation as God sends all of you as missionaries into the world around you?

Prayer

I pray you feel the wonder of Jesus' invitation to be more like Him. I pray you see the many ways this invitation gifts you to be a missionary in the places where you live—in your church, home, work, school, marketplace, and neighborhood. I pray you joyfully receive the call to become more like Christ, serve with brothers and sisters from your local assembly, and see the reality of God's work as His kingdom comes to the world around you.

In Jesus' name,

Amen

2 | *Abiding in Christ*

Gifted sculptors can "see" the potential of a block of wood or piece of marble. Some duck carvers, for example, say their craft is quite easy; all one has to do is cut away all that does not look like a duck. God's work to form us into new creatures has some removal aspects, but His work demonstrates the dynamic of living into our "new creatureliness" (II Corinthians 5:17).

The call to be re-formed in Christ's image comes with a number of different resources. Jesus' disciples differed substantially from disciples that follow other rabbis or philosophers. Jesus called His disciples; they did not select Him from the *Jerusalem Journal's* "Top Ten Rabbi" list for AD 30. Jesus also invited His disciples to an intimate relationship with Him and each other rather than to a body of sacred texts. In fact, Jesus freely found ways to depart from the received oral tradition. We see this tendency in Jesus' kingdom-shaped sermons where He states, "You have heard that it hath been said by them of old time . . . but I say unto you . . ." (Matthew 5:33–34). Since Jesus came to fulfill all the Law and prophets, He would obviously need to give a more complete meaning of the Law and various prophecies.

Spiritual formation provides the opportunity to develop new loves and habits with a definite goal in mind. Since Adam and Eve's sin and subsequent removal from the Garden of Eden, humanity has wrestled with many types of alternative gods. Sometimes these gods look like wood or stone statues, but at other times they look more like ideas such as liberty or power. Jesus shocked His original audience as well as readers today when He said, "Think not that I am come to send peace on earth: I came not to send peace, but a sword. For I am come to set a man at variance against his father, and the daughter against her mother, and the daughter in law against her mother in law. And a man's foes shall be they of his own household" (Matthew 10:34–36). As we follow Jesus, He identifies various idols as anything that comes between us and His ways.

Jesus knew the way to discipleship resulted more from faithfully following Him than just fleeing sinful and idolatrous practices. In *Our Home Is Over Jordan*, Homer Ashby[1] draws an excellent parallel between pastoral theology today and different outcomes of crossing the Red Sea and the Jordan River. When people of faith focus on leaving Egypt and its sin behind, they fail to purposefully move on to their God-given destiny.

Therefore, spiritual disciplines may look like efforts to get free from our old sinful ways rather than walking boldly as men and women of faith. Such efforts keep what is left behind as the referent or yardstick of growth rather than the One who calls us onto the mission with Him. While prayer, reading the Word, and serving others may still take a disciplined effort, they serve to transform our whole lives into His image where we too can be about the Father's business.

Personal Reflection

1. *What are two points in your walk as a disciple where you have seen Christ remove things that are not like Him?*

2. *After thinking about God's removal work, we have not finished the discipleship process. What are some ways the Teacher is calling you to be more like Him?*

3. *Share one or two of the ways God is working to bring this transformation to pass in your life with a spiritual friend.*

NORMAL DISCIPLES

Part of Jesus' Farewell Discourse in John's Gospel laid out the relationship we could have with Him, with each other, and with the world. We can only aspire to these relationships because Jesus has chosen and ordained us to bear fruit. Jesus described the relationship as an organic one: the Father oversees the process where the true vine (Jesus) and branches (abiding disciples) bear much fruit. Ultimately this fruitfulness witnesses to the world (John 15:27).

While Jesus' language may seem a little strange at first, He offers a relationship where certain fruits become normal. When compared to life separated from the vine, the normal abiding process may seem extreme, extraordinary, or even bizarre. In relationship with the Vine, however, productive branches celebrate a normal existence. Jesus alone sets the new norm or standard.

Perhaps readers may want to take the easier path and stop at this point. Many traditions of contemporary Christianity seek extraordinary life in Christ. Following Jesus does not offer such thrill-seeking or personally gratifying goals. Instead the abiding branches learn a new normal. This normal is so precious that they both welcome Jesus' description of the new normal and anticipate the Father's due diligence in pruning away all parts of life that do not contribute to fruitfulness. (See John 15:2.) Perhaps the disciples even joyfully anticipate the pruning process because the Father's loving care results in even greater fruitfulness.

Disciples celebrate leaving behind average human existence. Average results from comparing oneself or one's group to all other groups; being above or below average merely identifies one's place in the line of human behavior. Moving up the line still leaves a person in comparison to others. Disciples gain both their strength and prescribed norms from being in Jesus. They celebrate the wonderful gift of a new norm, a place where they can confidently live out their calling. They embrace life in Word and Spirit while turning from pragmatic, human-centered efforts to gain results.

Jesus' disciples reject extreme measures as unfaithful to the new norm. Perhaps Elijah's encounter with Baal's prophets illustrates the principle. Baal's prophets engaged in extreme practices throughout the day. Such practices included sweat and blood to no avail. Elijah, on the other hand, prayed a simple, normal prayer. The true prophet saw the sacrifice consumed.

Spiritual formation looks to the leading of Christ as found in the written Word and present in the Spirit. The process follows biblical practices to move more closely in line with the Rabbi's own habits and purposes to create our new normal. Such practices transform us to be more like Jesus.

Jesus came as a result of God's love for the world. Jesus gave His life to redeem all creation from the effects of sin. He carefully explained the shift from average living to His new norm. For example, Jesus spent a considerable amount of time calling His followers to release average desires to be masters of others with His new norm of being a servant (Matthew 20:25–28). He called for an attitude of forgiveness rather than seeking to get even or find retribution (Luke 6:35–38). Jesus offered a new normal in valuing relationships with Him over the old way of valuing treasures (Luke 12:16–21). Perhaps He could do so because He offers limitless love and sufficient grace in the place of limited resources such as gold or honor. Finally Jesus offered comfort and hope in God's plan and ability to perform rather than fear of the future and the unknown. Disciples treasure Jesus' voice above all other voices.

Spiritual formation gifts us with both the right goals and means to achieve the goals. While we can do nothing without Christ (John 15:5), in Him we can produce normal fruit—fruit that comes directly from the vine's resources. Intentionally abiding in Christ through the various formation strategies outlined in this book will prioritize the fruit chosen by Christ rather than goals valued in our fallen human condition.

Personal Reflection

1. *Why do you think humans gravitate toward more extreme methods in their efforts to get God's attention?*

2. *Compare extreme human efforts with Jesus' model prayer in Matthew 6 and the disciples' prayer for boldness in Acts 4.*

3. *What are some moments when you have tried to use extreme measures to get God's attention? How might you learn to rely more on God's gracious care than on earning what you need?*

FRUIT 1: ANSWERED PRAYER

Ironically, answered prayer does not actually start with praying or generating a prayer list. Spiritual formation centered on personal and community efforts to be like Christ must start with the relationship with the Teacher. Abiding in Jesus and His words precede asking. In Matthew 28:18–20 Jesus sets His agenda following the Crucifixion and Resurrection. As Jesus prepared to leave His disciples, He announced the reality of "all power . . . in heaven and in earth" being placed at His disposal. While we might choose to fix all wrongs or make people be good with that kind of power, Jesus chose to concentrate all of His universe-encompassing power on sending His people to make disciples. Abiding in Christ and having His words abide in us will radically change both our prayer attitude and prayer content as we will explore in chapter 5.

Abiding in Christ results in the fruit of answered prayer and the Father's glorification. All spiritual formation should emphasize abiding in Jesus and being completely saturated by His words. Such focus requires us to examine spiritual formation in all areas of life: fasting and service (chapter 6), thanksgiving and multiple aspects of our emotions (chapter 7), repenting and forgiving (chapter 8), simplicity and stewardship (chapter 9), work and leisure (chapter 10), Humility and Silence as we practice Jesus' presence (chapter 11), walking through seasons of loss and suffering (chapter 12), all forms of our communication (chapter 13), and corporate reflections through remembering and storytelling (chapter 14). While no one will be able to focus their efforts on more than two or three of these areas at one time, disciples will need to spend multiple cycles on these areas during their lifetimes. Bringing all of life to Christ through these disciplines enables us to confidently ask what we will and find our greatest pleasure in the Father's glorification (John 15:7–8). Being Jesus' disciple makes every step in spiritual formation worth the commitment!

Personal Reflection

1. *Praying flows from our life in Christ and His Word. Think about your last season in the Word or a church Bible study. What prayer request would naturally flow from your study?*

2. *Take a few moments and pray that prayer.*

3. *What attitudes or prayer practices might you change to be more fruitful in praying?*

4. *How do these proposed changes connect to being in Christ? How do they connect to serving on His mission in the world?*

FRUIT 2: ABIDING IN CHRIST'S LOVE

Spiritual formation enables us to experience Jesus' love and abide in that love. The spiritual formation disciplines explored in this book draw our attention from self-centered love to loving by obeying Jesus' commandments. All competing worldviews point to a different understanding of love. Temples of entertainment, politics, business, and human-centered learning preach a different kind of love.[2] Perhaps those loves rest in pleasure, happiness, self-satisfaction, accumulation of wealth and power, or leaving a personal legacy through professional accomplishments. Abiding in the true vine [3] provides strength to reject false loves and embrace love centered on discipleship obedience. Other forms of love do not flow from God.[4]

Our fallen nature does not lead us to obedience any more than it predisposes two-year-olds to love the word yes and resist saying no to a parent's directive. Spiritual formation calls us to remember the greatness of Christ's demonstrated love—a love willing to endure the cross by "despising the shame" before Him (Hebrews 12:2). Concerted effort to respond to God's enacted love frees us to flourish through obedience. When asked to identify the greatest commandment, Jesus agreed with the lawyer's summation, "Thou shalt love the Lord thy God with all thy heart, and with all thy soul, and with all thy strength, and with all thy mind; and thy neighbor as thyself"

(Luke 10:27). Loving like Jesus changes both the definition and object of love. We must love one another, even those neighbors that do not look or act like us. Abiding in Jesus centers us in obediently loving, even loving our enemies. (See Luke 6:32–35.)

Abiding in Christ calls all disciples to subvert selfishness with the Teacher's modeled love. Spiritual formation sets the disciples' course for following this central norm.

Personal Reflection

1. *Think about the way our world loves. How do you see the world's view of love in its songs, entertainment, and advertisements? How does this differ from Jesus' example?*

2. *How does Jesus' command differ from societal beliefs that people fall into love, cannot control love, and that people just have to follow their hearts?*

3. *What challenges do you face as God prunes away societal ideas and replaces them with Christ's norm of commanded love?*

4 *Discuss your responses with spiritual friends or a church small group. How can disciples help each other in uncovering unrecognized love attitudes from the world and replacing them with Jesus' command to love?*

Fruit 3: Lasting Joy

The frenetic rate of change inspired Alvin Toffler to write *Future Shock* in 1970. He believed the overwhelming changes modern people face would create a psychologically damaging state for individuals and societies. Only those who could learn a new literacy, the ability to adapt to change, could thrive in this new world. And we now think the 1970s represented a slower pace of life.

Evidently change is not the only cause for despair. Jesus named joy as a normal disciple fruit. Perhaps the culture of violence, poverty, animosity between various people groups, and unmanageable shame brought joylessness to Jesus' audience. Abiding in Christ changes all of that. Regardless of the sources of emotional turmoil, Jesus felt abiding in Him would make the conditions conducive for His joy to take root. In fact, Paul believed living out the kingdom of God created an opportunity where "righteousness, and peace, and joy in the Holy Ghost" would flourish (Romans 14:17).

Jesus created the conditions for lasting joy. We should remember Jesus used an agricultural metaphor to explain this relationship between abiding in Him and bearing joyful fruit. The *crop* of joy may take a period of time to come to harvest. Perhaps this is why Jesus said, "These things have I spoken unto you, that my joy might remain in you, and that your joy might be full" (John 15:11). Disciples have the wonderful privilege to receive Jesus' joy and await the fulfillment of that joy in their own lives. Readers lacking this fruit will need to intentionally pursue strategies for abiding in Jesus if they seek lasting joy. True joy, like true love, must come from the true vine.

The emotions of a normal disciple must include joy at its core. Emotional holiness will address challenges of fear, worry, anger, despair, and listlessness. A number of the disciplines in this book will call us to repent of abnormal emotional holiness and listening to the wrong voices in our lives. These efforts require being a part of Christ's body, the church, as well as having a personal relationship with Christ. As we can see from I Peter 5, humility comes in relationship with others as well as "the mighty hand of God." This humility provides the context for "casting all your care [anxiety] upon him; for he careth for you" (I Peter 5:7). Holding onto anxieties points toward a lack of humility and a less than optimal experience of abiding in Christ. Casting our cares on Christ liberates us for lasting joy.

Personal Reflection

1. *Identify areas of your life that seem to be out of control. How do these factors rob you of your joy?*

2. *How does the Bible's directive to live joyfully cause you to pray about those out of control areas?*

3. *How can this prayer help you receive Jesus' joy and become full of joy even when the sources of trouble are outside of your control? How might you include Paul's confession, "For I have learned, in whatsoever state I am therewith to be content" (Philippians 4:11)?*

CONCLUSION

Jesus' farewell conversation on normal disciple fruit may appear impractical or even impossible to us at times. Perhaps some readers experience discouragement before even examining the various spiritual disciplines outlined in the coming chapters. If disciplines mean our work, then this discouragement makes perfect sense. On the other hand, if abiding in Christ exists as the precondition of spiritual disciplines, then we will produce fruit. We can pray and receive answers to prayers in ways that glorify the Father, love in accordance with Jesus' commands, and grow in joy (John 15:18–19).

As disciples we find comfort and hope in the reality that Jesus has chosen us (John 15:16). Jesus calls us to discipleship as He did the original twelve apostles. They produced fruit, and so shall we. Bearing fruit of answered prayer, love, and joy is the Teacher's good pleasure for all of us. With this confidence we can turn to the wonderful opportunities awaiting us in spiritual formation.

Personal Reflection

Write a reflection on your blessings as a child of God. Include the beauty of producing Jesus-like fruit and the wonder of knowing that Jesus is overjoyed with your life. Consider sharing your reflection with a friend over a cup of coffee or post it on social media.

Prayer

I pray you flourish in all areas of your life as you abide in Jesus. I pray you realize again that He is the One who holds and secures you, who feeds you, who makes you produce lasting fruit. I pray the Word fuels your prayers with Kingdom-shaped imagination that unites your deepest desires with the Teacher's eternal will. I pray you experience more answered prayers that bring glory to God than you have ever experienced before. I pray the fruit of joy and love abounds in dimensions you never thought possible before. I pray the limits of that joy and love come from abiding in Christ rather than any circumstances around you.

In Jesus' name,
Amen

3 | *The Mission*

A postolic spiritual formation calls for a renewed look
at the end goal of spiritual disciplines. If Christ only
came to save sinners, then He would not have made disciples. He would have dutifully helped people see the error
of their ways, repent, and be ready for eternity. Rather
than preparing people for eternity, He brought eternity
to them. For example, Mark 1:14–15 summarizes the
Teacher's ministry by informing us that, "Jesus came into
Galilee, preaching the gospel of the kingdom of God, and
saying, The time is fulfilled, and the kingdom of God is at
hand: repent ye, and believe the gospel." Jesus presented
an incarnational gospel rather than an excarnational one.

Excarnational gospels and spiritual formation have
deep roots in American culture, the soil that gave birth
to major portions of the modern Pentecostal movement.
A mid-twentieth century song portrays this excarnational
view of the gospel. Rosemary Clooney's recording of
"This Ole House" reached number one on the US Bill-
board and UK Singles charts in 1954. The country music
songwriter Stuart Hamblen composed the song after finding an old prospector's body in a shack far from the nearest
Texas road. With its resigned refrain, "Ain't gonna need
this house no more," the song's metaphor of lacking time

to fix the house resonates with conservative Protestant-ism's anticipation of Christ's soon return.

This popular secular tune mirrors many sacred songs as well. For example, at first blush "Above All Else I Must Be Saved" seems to convey the right perspective. How-ever, Jesus taught His followers to pursue a much more inclusive goal—an incarnational one that calls to mission now and eternity with Him later. In fact in Jesus' high priestly prayer He strongly states, "I pray not that thou shouldest take them out of the world, but that thou shoul-dest keep them from the evil. . . . As thou hast sent me into the world, even so have I sent them into the world" (John 17:15, 18). Jesus' mission indeed was to seek and to save that which was lost (Luke 19:10). However, His discipleship call included them on His wider mission of reconciling all things to God.

Jesus' mission in the church equips us to be ambassadors for Him. Above all else we have the privilege to respond to Paul's plea, "Present your bodies a living sacrifice, holy, acceptable unto God which is your reasonable service" (Romans 12:1). God saved us to be living witnesses in this world. Above all else we must be faithful stewards of the gifts and commissions the Master has placed in our lives.

Personal Reflection

1. *How does a more comprehensive understanding of salvation that includes mission now and eternity with Christ later affect the meaning of "being saved?" How do your spiritual practices apply to both aspects of being saved?*

2. *How does your approach to discipling others change with this enriched understanding?*

EXAMINING DISCIPLESHIP GOALS

Jesus' disciples heard their Master proclaim the joyous truth of only one way to the Father. He told them He was the only way, truth, and the life (John 14:6). All other efforts could be classified as attempted theft (John 10:1). *Spiritual formation is the lifelong personal and communal commitment to know Christ, to be remade in His nature, and to be on His mission.* Following Christ calls for a reassessment of discipleship goals. Our Teacher continues to invite His disciples to live out His norms rather than being satisfied with only going to Heaven. He offers all of His followers this wonderful opportunity.

Spiritual formation solely in accordance with "This Ole House" and "Above All Else" can hinder the intended goal of being "Rapture ready." Spiritual formation does not earn our salvation or right standing with God. We are justified by faith. Salvation can only come as a free gift from a gracious, loving Savior. Any other perspective would cause disciples to boast in themselves rather than in Christ. The Galatian church had a concept of spiritual formation that tried to add works to grace. One can hear Paul's incredulous tone from nearly two millennia away, "Are you so foolish? Having begun in the Spirit, are ye now made perfect by the flesh?" (Galatians 3:3). Spiritual disciplines do not earn or secure our salvation; believing so would move us away from the grace of Christ unto another gospel "and would pervert the gospel of Christ" (Galatians 1:6–7). Christ did not die in vain.

Spiritual formation does not pursue the goal of greater status in the church. Being in Christ places us in the body where all members have a valuable role to play. Both Romans 12 and I Corinthians 12 help us realize the way the Lord graciously gifts His body. Competition for status represents behavior of those outside of Christ. In Christ the members mutually submit and give thanks for all of God's gracious gifts. Rather than gaining rank or status from spiritual formation, a perspective that deforms rather than transforms, Christ's disciples supply each other with the support they need. Spiritual formation destroys competition since it edifies the body in love (Ephesians 4:16). Following Christ results in more than merely stopping competition and other forms of abuse; instead disciples give to those in need (Ephesians 4:28). What a wonderful way to put on Christ!

Spiritual formation guides disciples away from the goal of "just doing more." Sometimes we more acutely recognize the need to draw closer to Christ when we feel low spiritually, experience a life crisis, or feel stuck in ministry. Unfortunately, our human condition defaults to solving our own problems by doing more things. If praying, serving, giving thanks, or other spiritual disciplines are not in place, then disciplines should certainly be added. Just praying more minutes or reading more chapters a day, however, is not sufficient to transform us into the image of Christ. The disciples, for example, noticed a real difference between their prayers and their Teacher's prayers. Consequently they asked for instruction in that specific discipline (Luke 11:1). As we will see in the remainder of this book, all spiritual disciplines lead to significant spiritual maturity as we become more like Christ—such maturity will impact our relationship with God, His people, and those who live around us. Spiritual formation intentionally seeks transformation rather than just being more disciplined.

The discipline of forgiveness provides an example of this principle. The need for forgiveness springs directly from sin's divisiveness. Christians can forgive because they have experienced God's forgiveness. As we repent, the Lord forgives us. Consequently, a broken relationship experiences restoration. As we forgive others, and ask for forgiveness when we have caused harm, our relationships experience healing. While we do need more forgiveness, the reality of practicing forgiveness, when properly understood, brings about spiritual maturity. (See chapter 8.) We become more like Christ.

Some people engage in spiritual formation as a quest for personal meaning or value. Like the "just do more" approach, searching for personal meaning fails to value the inherent relational aspect of spirituality. By definition, spiritual formation requires an awareness and development of relationship with God and His creation. If we find personal value in spiritual disciplines without relational maturity, then we would actually experience de-formation. We become less human when we lack relationships. The Gospels give an example of spiritual de-formation. One of Jesus' woes to the religious elite of His day indicted their missionary efforts to make a convert. They made the convert twice the "child of hell" he was before conversion (Matthew 23:15). Misguided spiritual disciplines de-form the practitioner.

While authentic spiritual formation does bring value to the saint, that is not the goal. Jesus criticized religious practices that led to status, personal value, or recognition. He went so far as to say, "Whosoever shall exalt himself shall be abased; and he that shall humble himself shall be exalted" (Matthew 23:12). As we shall see in chapter 11, Jesus' disciples practiced humility as a spiritual discipline; they did so in relationship with one another. In due time, God would be the One who would exalt or ascribe value to them. (See I Peter 5:5–6.)

Humbly examining spiritual formation goals should not induce anxiety or hinder the disciple's quest to be more like the Teacher. The wonder of humility includes the treasured possibility of "casting all your cares upon him; for he careth for you" (I Peter 5:7).

Personal Reflection

1. *This chapter examines several discipleship goals which fall short of Christlike transformation. Think back to a time when you experienced spiritual stagnation or decline. How were your spiritual goals off track at that time? What did or could you do to become more like Christ?*

2. *Think about your current spiritual and ministry needs. What is an example where just doing more prayer or Bible reading is not producing the results you want to see? How does adjusting the goal to becoming more like Christ and being on His mission change the dynamics of your situation? How could this focused goal change your prayer, Bible reading, and service?*

Invitation to Investing in the Kingdom

Looking back on the development of technology, a person may wonder what would happen if they had invested in the right stock offerings. For example, buying one hundred shares of Microsoft stock at the original offering would have placed $2,800 at risk. If all dividends went back into the stock, then that original investment would be worth a reported $2.49 million—an astonishing 88,892 percent return! Parents who bought their child $1,000 worth of Disney stock at birth in 1948 would certainly have helped that child retire at sixty-eight with about $96 million. When American Century Investments sold most of its stock to J. P. Morgan after forty years of business, the original $1,000 had grown to $600 million in 1998. The American Dream lives with these kinds of hopes and possibilities. Unfortunately, very few people experience the realization of such great financial success—the dream becomes a myth.

Spiritual formation, on the other hand, provides even greater dividends—dividends for both this life and the next. This calculation is not limited to the value of a person's soul. Jesus asked His disciples that all-important question in Matthew 16:26: "For what is a man profited, if he shall gain the whole world, and lose his own soul? Or what shall a man give in exchange for his soul?" While being saved is well worth the cost of taking up one's cross as explained by Jesus, spiritual formation provides an even higher dividend. This investment is no dream.

Spiritual formation invites us to go back to the beginning. In the Garden of Eden, God chose His own image as the model for men and women, and then He gave them the opportunity to collaborate with Him by multiplying, filling, and subduing the whole earth. Adam began the process by naming the animals he found on the exploratory journey for companionship. Adam and Eve had the commission to go beyond cataloging species to actually expanding the Garden to cover the earth! Their glory and honor included dominion over the works of the hands that had formed them—all beasts, all fowl, and all sea creatures (Psalm 8). This ground-floor assignment turned into an investment bust as the progenitors of the human race lost control of themselves and suffered expulsion from the very Garden their Maker had designed them to expand. What began with such great expectations ended with misery, failure, and helplessness where nothing could be found under human control (Hebrews 2:8). Humanity's stock potential continually finds depths of loss and pain. Fortunately, humanity did not create themselves or originate from some cosmic game of chance. We can now see Jesus come, suffer on our behalf, and bring many children to glory (Hebrews 2:10).

Like John the Baptist's audit team, we know Jesus is the Christ, and we have a spiritual mandate that exceeds what John held. The least in the Kingdom is greater than John. Jesus went even further in John 14:12: "He that believeth on me, the works that I do shall he do also; and greater works than these shall he do; because I go unto my Father." To miss the big picture of God's ground-floor investment would be far worse than the economic collapse in 2008 when US homeowners and stock market participants lost a total of $10.2 trillion, one-fifth of the world's gross domestic product that year. The American Dream crash pales in comparison to the loss the world experiences when God's people slip beneath His purposes

for the church. In spiritual formation we actively participate in the Kingdom coming to earth as it is in Heaven
(Matthew 6:10).

Personal Reflection

*The Book of Acts catalogs many Kingdom
advancement points. How did God use
common men and women of faith to bring
about His purposes? Can you identify ways they
became more like Christ? If Luke provided their
prayers, how did they pray? How did they use the
Old Testament or Jesus' teaching and ministry in their
prayers?*

GOD'S MISSION

Perhaps spiritual formation's potential can be seen in
God's consistent mission across the expanse of all Scripture. After saving humanity from total oblivion by the
faithfulness of shipwright-preacher Noah, God chose one
couple as the means to bless all families of the earth (Genesis 12:3). Abraham and Sarah's descendants went from
the wonder of witnessing God's redemptive work to only
doing "what was right in their own eyes." The missional
decline brought violence and suffering. (See Judges 21:25.)
Rather than crying out to the Lord like they did in Egyptian bondage, Israel petitioned for a king to judge them
"like all the nations" (I Samuel 8:5). They traded their
ground-floor investment in God's reclamation mission for
being like their neighbors.

God's plans for creation did not suffer derailment because of human failure. His mission continued unabated. He chose to make a covenant with King David to provide a son that would sit on the throne forever. The Temple provided a house of prayer for all people (Isaiah 56:7). David's sons followed the be-like-the-neighbor trajectory until the Lord used Assyria to destroy the Northern Kingdom and Babylon to do the same in the South.

God still did not discard His plan. Israel could be a witness in exile just as she should have been in the confederacy or the monarchy. The prophet gave the exiles an important word from the Lord. They continued to play a vital role in bringing peace to their cities of exile. In short, the one God of Israel wanted His people to be the restoration agents for all nations.

God's mission did not change with the Messiah's birth. Israel anticipated the birth of one who would sit on David's throne and would restore the nation to its former glory. This nationalistic tendency caused many people to place inappropriate expectations on Jesus. The disciples even continued to misunderstand Jesus' mission after His resurrection. They asked, "Lord, wilt thou at this time restore again the kingdom to Israel?" (Acts 1:6). They still viewed Jesus' mission as limited to Abraham's natural children. From the people's perspective, Jesus was just one more in a long line of messianic figures that failed to fulfill their expectations.

Jesus, however, would be both the child born to fulfill Isaiah's prophecy for the "Wonderful, Counsellor, The mighty God, The everlasting Father and The Prince of Peace" (Isaiah 9:6) and the prophet's dire prediction that "He was wounded for our transgressions, he was bruised for our iniquities: the chastisement of our peace was upon him; and with his stripes we are healed" (Isaiah 53:5).

Jesus resisted Israel's expectations. Rather than upholding family and nation as the center of God's messianic work, Jesus startled His followers by proclaiming, "Whosoever shall do the will of my Father which is in heaven, the same is my brother, and sister, and mother" (Matthew 12:50). Certainly Jesus' original audience assumed He limited "whosoever" to Israel; instead, very early in His ministry, He went to Israel's marginalized members such as tax collectors and lepers. He even intentionally traveled to Samaria to find the woman at the well who evidently had no family to support her. Jesus spoke lovingly to those caught in sinful situations while speaking harshly to those who used the Father's house for personal gain rather than as a place of prayer. That house of prayer was for all nations. At His departure, Jesus commissioned the followers to witness to the "uttermost part of the earth" (Acts 1:8).

Paul valued the role of Jewish priority while he was a missionary to the Gentiles. He claimed the gospel was to the Jew first and then to the Greek because the Jews had received God's words first. Yet Jewish failure to recognize their Messiah did not negate God's plans. As a devout Jew, Paul had to experience a radical worldview makeover similar to the apostle Peter. Peter's vision of God's reclassification of unclean animals to clean animals did not make much sense until the Holy Spirit interrupted his preaching in Cornelius's house (Acts 10:44). Once they received the Spirit, Peter baptized them in the name of the Lord.

God's mission clarification always brings legitimate questions from faithful people. Some Jerusalem believers expressed their concern that Peter had eaten with

Gentiles. After recounting his experience, the disputants changed their perspective; they glorified God as they realized God's work among the Gentiles. Then, as now, missional living requires a commitment to ongoing spiritual formation. Serving on God's mission allows Christians to celebrate the wonder of spiritual formation. Personal, local church, and even denomination-wide ministries will undergo changes over time. Such changes always demand laying aside some preferences and expectations in response to God's new work. God's mission never changes.

Personal Reflection

1. *This section examines God's missional faithfulness in both the Old and New Testaments. How can you see this reality in the Psalms? For example, how did psalms of lament (e.g., Psalm 22) aid Israel in seeing God's faithfulness in difficult times? How might a creation hymn such as Psalm 104 lead you and your discipleship group today?*

2. *View your life through either a biblical character or a psalm. What parallels do you see between the challenges and opportunities you face and those God's people faced in Scripture as they sought to live out God's missional calling?*

TO KNOW CHRIST

Participating in God's mission provides the wonderful opportunity to know Christ in ever deepening ways. Faithful men and women in Scripture accepted the invitation to hear God's voice and take steps into unknown areas. Spiritual formation today follows the same plan. While disciples may not know the exact consequences of taking steps of faith today, they confidently take those steps. This kind of confidence, also known as trust, only comes from an intimate relationship with Christ. Before disciples can follow Christ, they must be willing to confront spiritual barriers in their lives.

Even understanding Jesus' birth presents one of those barriers. The Incarnation features a scandal of unimaginable proportions. How in the world could the holy, creator God that preexisted everything become a human being? The problem existed for Jew and Greek alike. For Abraham's children, idolatry had trapped them so many times that they resisted any attempt to see representations of God. The failure at Sinai provided the first example. The ex-slaves had breathed so much Egyptian culture that they could not grasp the magnitude of the God who Moses met on the mountain. They made a golden calf and called it Yahweh. Judgment came. In the Promised Land they had to learn agricultural sciences from the Canaanite inhabitants. They failed to separate crop planting and harvesting from Baal and Astarte worship. Judgment came. King David's sons often failed to remove the high places, ancient cultic sites, even when they restored some ele ments of faithful Yahweh worship. Judgment came. By the time of Christ, the Jewish people had learned this difficult lesson—any hint of idolatry suffered instant rejection. When Jesus forgave the paralytic man in Mark 2, the scribes immediately saw a national threat: "Why doth this man thus speak blasphemies? Who can forgive sins but God only?" (Mark 2:7).

The Greek mind saw God as some immovable force. As dualists they believed spirit and matter represented two forms of existence, and spirit was far superior to matter. The material world only crudely represented the ideas behind them. For God to touch matter, as in the Incarnation, a junior god or angel of some kind would have to serve as an intermediary being. The Incarnation would not exist in the Greek mind—too much space existed between pure spirit and tangible matter.

The Cross presented another challenge for Jewish and Greek theology as Paul noted in I Corinthians 1:21–31. The Old Testament cursed people who hung on a tree (Deuteronomy 21:22–23; see also Galatians 3:13). Greeks could not abide the foolish paradox of a dead savior. To know Christ required both Jews and Greeks to throw away their preconceived ideas and accept Christ as He presented Himself to them. As we see in Paul's pointed attack of Judaizers in Galatians, some believers had severe difficulties in giving up their own ideas and efforts. Paul himself sought to know Christ and "the power of his resurrection, and the fellowship of his sufferings, being made conformable unto his death" (Philippians 3:10). Spiritual formation opens the door to know Christ as we live out His mission.

Personal Reflection

1. *God always calls His people to carefully examine failures or idols of culture around them. Consider key elements of national or local culture that you breathe every day. What are some of the idols that so easily*

detract the church from its mission (for example,
nationalism, individualism, materialism, etc.).

2. *What are some ways you have battled these*
   cultural realities? How does the Bible provide
   wisdom to confront these idols? How does this
   wisdom help you and the church know and follow
   Christ more faithfully?

CONCLUSION

As we respond to Jesus' invitation to follow Him, we too will encounter significant challenges to both our understanding and our faith. We must trust that the One who came, suffered, died, and rose again will be present with us as we take steps into new possibilities. Such unknown steps will only happen by faith. As with the New Testament believers, we will be confronted at the very core of our belief system from time to time. Anything short of radical transformation into the image of Christ is a shadow of the wonderful purpose God has for His people.

PRAYER

I pray the Lord gives you the courage to place His purposes firmly at the top of your spiritual formation goals. I pray the Spirit gives you a renewed passion for the Kingdom to be on earth as it is in Heaven. I pray for increased spiritual blessings in your life and the local congregation where you worship. I pray every effort to love people in the broken world around you bears results according to God's plan. I pray you never grow weary with well doing and in your faithful service you will know the joy of the Lord in a new dimension.

In Jesus' name,
Amen

4 | *Worship, Baptism, and Communion*

As a child I enjoyed finger plays and rhymes along with many preschoolers. A common finger play defined the church for many of us: "Here is the church, here is the steeple, look inside, and here's all the people." Many people continue to identify the church with a building, worship service times, and programs designed to address felt human needs. While churches sometimes have buildings, sometimes have published worship times, and sometimes develop formal programs to address problems, none of these things actually define the church. For example, the church's early years saw tremendous growth without owning any property. Modern missionaries, whether they go to urban centers in North America or Islamic countries where they cannot legally have a church, celebrate the wonderful truth that churches can flourish without buildings.

Perhaps the church represents another "manna" reality. God provided Israel on-time sustenance in the desert with an unnamed food. Israel just began to call it, "What is it?" Manna identified something beyond normal experience. Saints seeking lifelong development as disciples must do so in the context of God's people. For the church to be a witness to the world, members of the church must mature together. As such, a large portion of church leadership

45

responsibility can be seen in the mandate to equip the saints for their work of ministry (Ephesians 4:11–16).

This chapter explores the role of the church as an agent of spiritual formation for its members. The church provides guidance for developing relationships, worship, living a baptized life, and receiving the Lord's Supper together. The discussion builds upon the vital reality of new birth, in which men and women have experienced initial conversion. As local church communities live out these priorities, they see Jesus "from whom the whole body fitly joined together and compacted by that which every joint supplieth, according to the effectual working in the measure of every part, taketh increase of the body unto the edifying of itself in love" (Ephesians 4:16).

PAUL'S PERSPECTIVE

Spiritual formation draws heavily from the apostles who laid the foundation of the church. Paul interpreted his missionary calling to the Gentiles as a continuation of Jesus' work of reconciling "in the body of his flesh through death, to present you holy and unblameable and unreproveable in his sight" (Colossians 1:22). Paul's own work was to preach Christ, "warning every man, and teaching every man in all wisdom; that we may present every man perfect in Christ Jesus" (Colossians 1:28).

The oneness theme plays a unifying role in Paul's letters. The Apostolic church readily sees and celebrates the oneness of God in the epistles, but the oneness of Christ's body does not gain the same attention. Spiritual formation pursues being remade in the image of Christ by the right relationship with the Father and by the empowering work of the Spirit. Spiritual formation must also attend to Jesus' prayer request that the people would be one even as He and the Father are one. The church that is "made perfect in one" plays a vital role in letting everyone know that the Father lovingly sent Jesus into the world. (See John 17:21–23.)

Paul also explored divisions in the body in some of his letters. The church at Corinth provides plenty of case studies on division. Divisions in the church demonstrated the need for additional spiritual formation as people transitioned from their pagan identity into their status as saints, people made holy with a purpose. They had already been baptized; they just were not living like it.

Identity in the ancient world came from gender, genealogy, and geography, according to Bruce Molina and Jerome Neyrey. Rather than having a fully developed sense of "self" as experienced in modern western cultures, people living in biblical times found their identity and evaluated the identity of others through stereotypes of social and geographical locations.

As people entered the Corinthian church, they had to find a new identity to replace the one left behind. New converts would make errors in becoming new creatures in relationship with each other. Consequently, people found value in wealth, the personality of leaders, and even in spiritual gifts exhibited in their congregations. In I Corinthians 13, Paul called all members to surrender their personal identity quests to the abiding principles of faith, hope, and love. Inappropriate celebration of speaking in tongues, knowledge, faith, and sacrificial giving did not help the church members gain their new identity; without love these behaviors were no more than "sounding brass, or a tinkling cymbal." In the middle of his exposition of spiritual gifts, Paul had to relocate the saints' identities in selfless love.

We should anticipate challenges in church life today. Rather than being surprised or shocked by failures in the church, we see the possibility of renewing our identity in Christ like Paul did. He identified this divided group of people as "the church of God which is at Corinth, to them that are sanctified in Christ Jesus, called to be saints" (I Corinthians 1:2). We should only be surprised when we refuse to engage in the spiritual formation necessary to press toward our corporate identity in Christ. Rather than being discouraged, we can become "laborers together with God"—laborers that are God's garden and God's building (I Corinthians 3:9). As we will see later in this chapter, corporate worship, baptism, and communion provide examples of apostolic spiritual formation for everyone in the local congregation.

Personal Reflection

1. *What do you think was the major cause of division in the Corinthian church? Develop your ideas after locating a few challenges Paul addressed in his letter to that church. (Note: Paul wrote to the problem at the congregational level rather than addressing individuals with a failure.)*

2. *What are two or three ways you have grown spiritually by worshiping and fellowshiping with other saints? How does this process make you more like Christ?*

DEVELOPING IN RELATIONSHIPS

Both new birth and adoption convey the reality of becoming part of a new family. As we saw above, the early church consisted of people who came from different social positions on their way to becoming the bride of Christ. We may be tempted to view the church as a collection of Christian families. This approach parallels a social and political theory that says governments rule by the consent of the people. While this philosophy helped break the control of monarchs in Western Europe and their new world colonies, this perspective does not reflect the new social and spiritual organism called the church.

Jesus' disciples left their fishing boats and aging fathers behind when they accepted Christ's call. Jesus identified His family as those who do the Father's will (Matthew 12:48–50). Following Jesus required, and still requires, a commitment to lay down all other preferences and take on a new identity as a living sacrifice. Such extensive transformation demands a literal remapping of the mind (Romans 12:1–2). Modern neuroscience research confirms Paul's suggestion in Philippians 4:8 that thinking on honest, just, pure, lovely, virtuous, and praiseworthy things remaps the mind.

Dedicating one's life to Christ places the saint in Christ and His body. We are no longer our own, we have been bought with a price. We glorify God with all aspects of our lives. Becoming a member of this new body requires a total commitment to following God as new children. Paul systematically deconstructed the old way as he rebuilt the church to live in a manner acceptable to the Lord. (See Ephesians 5.)

Paul's guidance for living as new creatures provides an interesting phenomenon in the apostle's order of attention. He addressed life together in Christ before addressing household behaviors. This pastoral approach calls for spiritual formation in the church prior to considering life in the household. People who live out thanksgiving and mutual submission in the body will have no difficulty living this out in the home. In other words, Christian homes consist of saints rather than churches being an aggregate of nuclear families. Of course, the church extends far beyond what happens in gathered times of worship, as we discussed above. This wonderful truth also provides space for unmarried, widowed, and divorced saints, as well as those who live in nuclear families.

Disciples live their calling in a wide range of relationships: families, friendships, schools, and workplaces. Their spiritual formation must be applied in those various contexts. When disciples fail, they repent and receive forgiveness from one another, as we will see in chapter 8. While worship, preaching, fellowship, and prayer in the corporate gathering teach and encourage spiritual fruit, learning to cultivate the fruit of Galatians 5:22–23 requires attention to all relationships. Such growth requires accountability to other saints. As we experience spiritual growth in the context of personal relationships, we strengthen the church and its mission in the world.

Personal Reflection

Paul firmly believed elders should mentor and guide others in the church. What are two or three ways your life and ministry help to disciple others? Provide examples inside and outside of the corporate church setting.

CORPORATE WORSHIP

Perhaps the quintessential spiritual formation act is the corporate call to worship. Some theological traditions go so far as to say worship is the sole duty of humanity. As Apostolic Pentecostals we believe worship plays a vital role in our individual and collective walks of faith. We also anticipate the eternal worshipful state when we see Jesus face-to-face. (See I John 3:1–3.) While worship reorders every aspect of our lives, as sons and daughters we must live between our new birth and the final moment when "we shall be like him."

In her book, *Reaching Out without Dumbing Down*, Marva Dawn identifies elements of authentic worship. Dawn's elements of encountering God, forming Christian character, and building Christian community take us deeper into the nature of corporate worship. Apostolics, however, must go a step further in participating with God as He brings the Kingdom's reign into its full glory. We pray for the Kingdom to come (Matthew 6:10), and we participate in the work of Christ by "witnessing unto him" throughout the whole earth (Acts 1:8).

Corporate worship transforms people of faith as they daily live out their new character and identity. The author of Hebrews reminds us that we only have one worship leader, our High Priest who serves as the "minister of the sanctuary." We place our lives in His hands so He has something to offer when He goes into the true tabernacle. Jesus calls the church to worship. He invites us. He makes the way for us. All other doors to worship represent the paths of thieves and robbers. He not only calls us to worship, He also speaks through His Word. Jesus gives space to respond in communion and in altar-call commitments as ways to prepare us for service in the world.

Following the guidance of our worship leader requires us to tip over every form of idolatry. Rather than forgetting about our daily family, work, leisure, and social routines, we bring every aspect of our lives to the worship service. Presenting ourselves as living sacrifices is pleasing to God and is our reasonable service (Romans 12:1). Offering our lives to God provides the wonderful opportunity for the heavenly metallurgist to burn away all impurities. In worship the Father purifies us for His purposes (Isaiah 1:25).

Unfortunately, not all worship glorifies God. The New Testament records many examples of churches that did not worship well. The church of Corinth suffered from any number of schisms. James's scattered church suffered from the effects of war and lusts to the extent that they either did not pray or their prayers went unanswered. In fact disingenuous worship threatened the church in a way that the council's gag order failed to do—the Holy Spirit slew false worshipers. On the other hand, humble prayer brought a fresh move of the Spirit in Acts 4. James called the church to anoint the sick and confess their faults to one another if they wanted healing. Earnest prayer of righteous people still "avails much."

Personal Reflection

1. *How has corporate worship helped you identify areas in your life that needed transformation? Give a specific example. How did you continue to develop in line with the Spirit's work in the worship service? What resistance did you have to overcome in the process?*

2. *How does worship draw a congregation together in spite of, or because of, its great diversity (cultural, generational, social class, education level, etc.)?*

3. *How do you hear the Spirit speak through others in this process?*

BAPTIZED LIFE

Baptism has always played a significant role in the lives of Jesus' disciples. Some of His disciples started their spiritual journey under the ministry of John the Baptist. For John, baptism called for radical preparation for the coming Messiah. Baptism included faith, repentance, and commitment to a transformed life. Evidently, John's baptism deeply influenced his followers even though they had a limited amount of time to hear his preaching and follow his example. A couple decades after John's martyrdom, he still had followers seeking to live out their baptism in Ephesus. Paul sought to build on that baptism of repentance rather than dismantle it. They would need to move from repentance to other parts of new birth to become members of Christ's body.

Jesus began His public ministry with baptism. He overrode John's protest because baptism served to "fulfil all righteousness" (Matthew 3:15). Signs from above, the Spirit of God descending like a dove, and the voice declaring the Father's pleasure accompanied Jesus' baptism. Immediately following His baptism, the Teacher entered a season of spiritual formation in the wilderness. Baptism provided the context for the formal start to resisting Satan's temptations so the Kingdom could be proclaimed in His first message (Matthew 4:17).

Jesus included baptism in a postresurrection commissioning ceremony. He sent His followers to make disciples—a process that included baptism and teaching to observe all that Jesus commanded (Matthew 28:19–20). The apostles quickly followed Jesus' command when they baptized three thousand on the Day of Pentecost. As Peter stated, this was for the remission of sins. Repentance, baptism, and infilling of the Spirit all represent significant elements in the early stages of a transformed life.

Baptism does not end with conversion. While Christians do not practice repetitions of baptism (as did other religious sects in the first century), Christians do believe baptism has an ongoing effect in their lives. Paul emphasizes at least four effects or elements of baptism: a sign of the new covenant, the key to breaking sin's power, abiding relationship in Christ's body, and the testimony of the coming Resurrection and its conclusion with all corruption being put away.

Baptism's sign of the new covenant significantly influences spiritual formation. (See Colossians 2–3.) Disciples enter this covenant with God by being buried with Christ in baptism so they can be risen with Him. God forgives the sins of those baptized and nailed evidence of their guilt to the cross. Initial forgiveness by itself could cause people to see baptism as an event with little daily impact. Paul had a different perspective. Baptism rejects legalism and angel worship as means to live out our relationship in Christ. Instead, baptism's burial with Christ calls disciples to "set . . . affections on things above, not on things on the earth" (Colossians 3:2). In the remainder of the chapter Paul emphasized corporate and household behaviors that require a commitment to living in light of baptism. For example, a baptized life will demonstrate love's bond of perfectness, peace, and thankfulness (Colossians 3:14–15). The community of baptized disciples commits themselves to spiritual formation in these overarching principles. Living in Christ makes this possible.

Paul saw baptism as the pivotal point of conversion that breaks the power of sin and enables disciples to live freed from sin. Baptized disciples cannot continue in sin as a means to celebrate God's grace. Instead they are freed from sin and freed to live in Christ. Baptism calls disciples to evaluate their faithfulness in this new way of life. Holy disciples daily put away sinful behaviors and live with incarnational intentionality.

Unfortunately, many people see baptism as an individual event, much like the way evangelicals "accept Jesus" as their "personal Savior." Individuals are baptized, but they are not baptized by themselves. Baptism places disciples in both Christ and His body. Galatians 3:27–29 explores this impact of baptism. To accept one aspect of baptism requires accepting the other: baptism into Christ causes us to put on Christ, and we are all one in Christ Jesus.

Baptism into Christ removes all the things that created a separate identity. Paul specifically addressed categories of identity transformation for his audience: "There is neither Jew nor Greek, there is neither bond nor free, there is neither male nor female." The chasm between the sides of these three divisions cannot be overemphasized. While our culture seeks to dissolve gender distinctions by placing gender construction in individual choices and preferences, baptism into Christ removes the power differentials in community rather than as individual choices. Spiritual formation in community will identify barriers between various groups of people and replace these critical fractures with purposeful unity in Christ.

Finally, spiritual formation of baptized believers includes an eschatological focus. Just as disciples identify with Jesus in death, they will resurrect with Him! Jesus' resurrection is not complete until all corruption has put on incorruption; only then will death have truly lost its sting. As a consequence, Paul identified two specific elements of spiritual formation: baptized disciples (1) give thanks for the victory that comes through Jesus, and (2) remain steadfast in their work for the Lord because the Resurrection guarantees their labor is not in vain. (See I Corinthians 15:54–58.) Being a part of the baptized body of Christ rejects all divisiveness from the old life and enables the church to unify around the Teacher's mission. Baptism continues to change us.

Personal Reflection

1. *Reflect on your own baptism. What do you remember about that wonderful moment in your transition to a life in Christ? How can the wonder of baptism continue to give you power over sin today?*

2. *How have you seen someone else change in baptism? How was that person's experience similar to yours? How did it differ? How can you help adolescents and young adults appropriate baptism from their childhood? How do you respond to a returning backslider who asks to be baptized again?*

3. *What are some implications of being one
   baptized people? How might our unity in
   baptism prepare us to be peacemakers and offer
   the hope of unity to the world?*

COMMUNION

While baptism places all disciples in one body, the
Lord's Supper sets the table for that body. When we par-
take of bread and cup, we commune with the first disciples
who ate with Christ, as well as the untold millions who
have done so since that time. We commune with brothers and sisters from around the world today—some who
freely celebrate in public worship and others who take the
elements in silence because of oppressive governmental
policies. One body eats one bread.

Unfortunately, many people today see communion as
a time to forget about everyone else and focus on their
personal, individual relationship with the Savior. The
early church believed differently. Paul used the practice of
the Lord's Supper to bring unity to a divided church that
struggled with differences of opinions and practices about
how best to represent holy, incarnational living. "The cup
of blessing which we bless, is it not the communion of the
blood of Christ? The bread which we break, is it not the
communion of the body of Christ? For we being many are
one bread, and one body: for we are all partakers of that
one bread" (I Corinthians 10:16–17).

In the next chapter Paul would need to address some
abuses in celebrating the Lord's Supper. The abuses related
to the divisiveness seen throughout the whole epistle.
Taking the cup and bread of unity while arguing and

judging one another brought shame to Christ's sacrifice. Just as Old Testament priests suffered when they misused sacrifices, divided believers that abuse the sacrifice of Christ place themselves in danger of judgment. Paul said some saints suffered sickness and weakness because of this abuse (I Corinthians 11:30).

Rather than considering the meal as a threat to individual health, the Lord calls all to eat at the same table. He calls us to share in His body and blood together as we purposefully respond to the invitation to relationship and mission in the world. The Lord's Supper powerfully feeds spiritual formation for those who hunger and thirst after righteousness. Considering Jesus' example as He instated the four acts of His Supper can assist the body in pursuing God's purposes.

ACT 1: JESUS TOOK THE BREAD

On a previous occasion of multiplying bread, the disciples came unprepared to feed the crowd. They had to "borrow" a little boy's lunch. In this case Peter and John had the privilege of preparing for the Passover. In effect they set the table even though they were struggling with seeking personal privilege and status. Fortunately, Christ welcomes us to the table even though we still need healing in our spirit and reconciliation in our relationships.

Jesus still receives what we bring to the table. As we saw earlier in the worship discussion, Jesus serves as the High Priest. He receives what we bring and transports it to the Holy Place. When saints gather in communion they bring their best even as Jesus gave His best. Jesus receives our offering.

The act of corporately giving and receiving brings spiritual formation to the whole body. On any given Sunday, thousands of faith communities gather to receive the meal. Each congregation may face different spiritual maturity needs; each congregation may face different missional opportunities. The one bread makes them all one body.

ACT 2: JESUS GAVE THANKS

After Jesus received the bread, He gave thanks or blessed that which He received. Certainly, all believers and communities wish they could more faithfully respond to Jesus' invitation to ministry. Many come to the table with more questions than answers on how to go forward in times of suffering or confusing situations in the world. Those questions and flaws do not prevent the Teacher from blessing the meal. He only asks us to give what we have so He will have something to bless.

At times we feel ashamed of what we offer. How could we ever give in accordance with what we have received? How can we come when we know we could have lived a little better, served a little more cheerfully, prayed a little more faithfully, and loved a little more selflessly? We give what we have, and Jesus blesses. Remember Jesus' words in Peter's rooftop vision: "What God hath cleansed, that call not thou common" (Acts 10:15). When we place our lives in Jesus' hands, our fragments become uncommonly blessed by the Teacher. He makes us ready to participate in His mission in the world.

ACT 3: JESUS BROKE THE BREAD

Spiritual formation calls us to trust Jesus. As we have seen earlier, the Father prunes productive branches so they may produce even more fruit. The Father chastises those

He loves (Hebrews 12:6). His strength is made perfect in our weakness (II Corinthians 12:9). In fact, God takes things which others mean for evil and transforms them for a good outcome such as "to save much people alive" (Genesis 50:20). Christ's body suffered fracturing for the good of all the world. In the meal we receive His brokenness and feel His nail-pierced hands on our brokenness. In the meal we express our trust in the Teacher's ability to work all "for good to them that love God, to them who are the called according to his purpose" (Romans 8:28).

Some churches call the Lord's Supper the blessing or Eucharist. Most of us feel comfortable calling it communion. No church invites people to the Fracture or Breaking. Spiritual formation calls men and women of faith to hear His voice and become more like Him in crushing times of sorrow.

ACT 4: JESUS SHARED THE BREAD

Baptism positioned us in Christ and His mission in the world. The final act of the meal prepares us to be shared with each other and the world. As we saw in the worship section, all that the Teacher does in our lives prepares us for His purposes in the world. Disciples exist to follow the Teacher's example. Spiritual formation celebrates communion as a key means to reorient all of our lives toward the moment of sharing. Rather than, "Above all else I must be saved," communion calls us to say and believe, "Above all else I must be shared." Jesus came to share Himself with us. Now He sends us to be shared with the world. Our moments of breaking take on new hope and possibilities if we remember Christ prepares us to more effectively share ourselves with others.

Personal Refelction

1. *Imagine you were preparing to take communion in church tomorrow. How would each of the four acts help you receive the body and blood of Christ? How does this make you more like Christ?*

2. *How do the four acts unify one body with one bread in their one purpose to make disciples in all of the world?*

CONCLUSION

God's people have gathered in many different settings through the years. The apostles taught and led worship in schools, synagogues, houses, and in tentmaking workshops. Under communism's oppression, one African church would worship in the wilderness at times while at other times they would gather in small groups embedded in throngs of soccer fans—while the fans worshiped the athletes on the field, the disciples worshiped the Creator of all things. Workers join together during lunch breaks in factories to celebrate God's goodness. Saints worship at a graveside when they commit their loved ones to the Teacher's hands. They hear the vows of new husbands and wives in worship so they can help them stay faithful to those vows in the future. They welcome new converts to the family by the riverside.

Regardless of the location and exact rhythm of the liturgy, worship transforms the worshipers. By living in the Way together, they fellowship with one another, keep the apostles' doctrine, celebrate the Lord's Supper, and pray. Worship still results in signs and wonders, sharing resources, gladness, and favor with the people. A worshiping people participate in the Teacher's daily additions to the church. (See Acts 2:42–47.)

PRAYER

I pray the completeness of the Lord's body be found in your local church as well as the global church. I pray your worship transforms each gathering into a temple of the Spirit—a place where He dwells, where He saves, where He restores all the years destroyed by caterpillars and cankerworms, and a place where He sends you into new white fields of labor. I pray every division in the body experiences healing. I pray renewed fervor for the taught and preached Word. I pray for heartfelt service to fellow believers and the needy in the community. I pray every idol falls. I pray the Lord adds to the church daily.

In Jesus' name,

Amen

5 | *The Word and Prayer*

Often a large distance separates the power supply from the point of need. My home's electrical wiring does not measure up to the need for multiple outlets on every wall; I need to use extension cords to bridge the gap and meet my needs. Most buses have engines that generate power in the front, but they use their back tires to push the bus down the highway; a transmission and long drive shaft fill the gap. On October 9, 1936, engineers threw the switch to take power from the Hoover Dam in Nevada to light the city of Los Angeles 266 miles away. A mountain of concrete (enough to pave a four-foot sidewalk belt around the earth at the equator), towering generators (seventeen weighing four million pounds each), and seemingly endless transmission wires (2,700 miles) transform and relocate power from the Colorado River to California's largest city.

Power projects such as the Hoover Dam require a tremendous amount of labor. A total of twenty-one thousand men worked on the dam during its five years of construction with a peak employment of 3,500 a day in June 1934. Some paid the ultimate price to complete such a project in the allotted time. The dam project saw ninety-six deaths due to industrial accidents. Worthy projects also require an uncanny ability to withstand overwhelming pressures—at its base the Hoover Dam must handle forty-five thousand pounds per square foot of pressure!

The Hoover Dam looks like a child's Tinker Toy set compared to the missionary power needs the church encounters every day. The Master sends us to be salt, light, and a city on a hill for every people group in the world. On the one hand He sends us as defenseless lambs among wolves, but on the other hand all the power of the universe exerts its efforts on this one task of sending the church into the world to make disciples. While disciples do not generate the power, they must be skilled in accessing and participating in transmitting the power to the point of need.

God chose to invite His people into the task of reconciling the world unto Himself. Perhaps the primary means of participating in this wonderful opportunity rests in receiving the Word and praying for the Kingdom to come and God's will to be done. These twin activities serve as primary resources both by being the starting point and the most important avenue of participating in God's restoration work. As with all spiritual formation, these two disciplines transform the disciple rather than represent time-on-task assignments. This chapter will serve as an introductory guide to walking in Word and prayer. Through continued practice, individuals and local church communities have the opportunity to mature in both disciplines.

The harvest field demands it.

All other efforts fall woefully short of the power demands that disciples face.

As you read through this chapter, consider the relationship between your confidence in the Word and your willingness to pray Kingdom-focused prayers. Compare your prayer life with Paul's examples. Finally, anticipate a new power surge as you grow as a disciple through the Word and prayer.

THE AUTHORITY OF THE WORD

I assume readers of this book are familiar with the Bible and believe it has authority in their lives. Rather than presenting an apologetic explanation designed to convince the uncommitted or skeptical person, I hope to deepen your commitment to the Word as the source of authority in your life and open the potential of deepening your joy in actively strengthening your relationship with God through His Word.

Scripture begins with the power of the spoken Word. After a brief setup where the Spirit moves upon the face of the waters, God spoke the creation of energy: "Let there be light." Genesis 1:3 concludes with the impact of God's speech: "And there was light." While many of us would like a little more information to abiding questions such as how this light existed prior to the creation of the lights in firmament on the fourth day (Genesis 1:14), we must not move too quickly past the power of a simple, divinely imperative sentence and the creation of light.

John seems to follow a similar trajectory as he begins his Gospel. The Word was in the beginning with God, the Word made all things, and the Word generated unstoppable light (John 1:1–5). God enfleshed that Word (John 1:14) so He could dwell with us. Grace and truth burst into the human condition in a new way.

Paul encouraged Timothy to remember the powerful inspiration behind "all Scripture." We quickly read the fourfold profitability of Scripture and its maturing impact on the reader without remembering the context of this section of the letter. (See II Timothy 3:16–17.) In this chapter, Paul gave an unvarnished assessment of the evil that would assault the world in the last days. Paul's list accurately reflects newspaper and website headlines today; he starts his list with lovers of self, covetous, boasters, and pride. The corrupted human condition leaves people susceptible to forms of godlessness that fuel the lust.

Spirit without the authority of the Word transforms sinful human beings into even lower levels of existence. Paul's words echo Jesus' critique of scribes and Pharisees in Matthew 23. Pseudo-spirituality, human efforts to control God's work, creates even worse forms of hypocrisy. Trying to light a world by starting with the needs of the darkened world provides a paradoxical situation. Rather than giving life and light, building without the power of the Word guarantees the efforts will end in failure when storms come. On the other hand, building on the sayings of Jesus, both hearing and doing them will provide an indestructible house on the Rock. Jesus believed building without His words makes the fall greater than if we left people spiritually homeless.

Spiritual formation in the Word transforms people from unskillful babies to mature disciples who make a habit out of exercising their senses to know the differences between good and evil—an exercise that finds its root in the word of righteousness (Hebrews 5:12–14). Hebrews 6 reminds us of the desperate need of teachers who go beyond the foundational principles in God's Word (repentance, faith, baptism, laying on of hands, resurrection, and judgment) to the mature place where God can fulfill His multiplication promises in the church today. Sadly, the same chapter tells the consequences of not maturing in the Word. Those who linger in the basic essentials risk tasting the good Word only to fall away. Ultimately, they shame Christ. They will find themselves in the refuse heap awaiting the flames.

Disciples make themselves conformable to the Word. Rather than trying to discover a new vision for their lives or the lives of those entrusted to their care, they go back to the Word for light. "Where there is no vision, the people perish; but he that keepeth the law, happy is he" (Proverbs 29:18). Disciples need vision and light to illuminate their path; they also know the source of that light. Spiritual formation in the Word enables us to know and do the Word. Spiritual formation reminds disciples that obeying the Word serves a more critical role than sacrifice—worship without the Word's anchor (I Samuel 15:22).

Pentecost always has an experiential component. But experience does not provide the foundation of Pentecost. Pentecostal disciples must know and obey the Teacher. Knowing and doing the Word transforms people into Christ's image. They realize studying and following the Word may be the most critical components of worship. Since all saints have a role to fulfill in Christ's body, they will pursue a relationship with Christ through both the written Word and living Word present in the Holy Spirit.

Unfortunately, many people use difficult passages or areas of perceived contradiction to excuse themselves from following those which they *can* grasp. As a wise man once said, "We should be more troubled by the 95 percent of the Bible that we can understand and do not follow than the 5 percent we do not understand."

Personal Reflection

1. *Think about a time when you wrestled with a biblical principle. What helped you to respond faithfully to the Word's authority?*

2. *Is there an area where the Word is challenging you right now? Take some time to discuss the challenge with another believer.*

ACTIVELY READING THE WORD

The Word calls disciples to actively study Scripture. Their study, however, must go beyond a mere cognitive process. Western readers frequently assume reading can be kept separated from who we are and become as persons. Spiritual formation in the Word does not consist of reading a certain number of chapters each day or reaching a time goal. While creation had no option but to respond to God's Word, human beings have to consciously respond to the Word.

Edward Wimberly calls this process privileging God's conversations. Rather than constantly confronting messages from our fallen world and personal old nature, disciples must learn to let God's voice set the tone in everything they do. This privileging process happens through actively reading the Word, praying, listening to the Spirit, and fellowshiping with brothers and sisters. Corporate worship wonderfully assists believers in hearing the Word, elevating God over all other things in life, and caring for one another. These three corporate worship experiences strengthen disciples' resolve to take additional steps of daily living the Word.

Actively reading the Word approaches the Bible with a transformational commitment. The Word always moves us from living in the world to being a part of the gathered believers for the purpose of witnessing in the world. All other uses of the Word fall into some category of misuse or idolatry.

This understanding helps disciples approach Bible reading with the correct attitude and expectations. For example, disciples often encounter losses and grief in their spiritual journey. Scripture should play a significant role in dealing with a season of lament. Psalms of lament and passages about God's care for His people address all three of the movements mentioned above, rather than just making the person feel better. Scripture will take a disciple away from worldly or mere human efforts to solve the crises. Baptism firmly roots the believer in Christ's own suffering, rather than avoiding the loss, or nurturing feelings of victimization, abandonment, or even hatred of God. These immature responses call us to the Word; the Word brings much needed correctives in dealing with the loss.

The Word reminds suffering disciples they do not experience loss alone. The Book firmly places suffering in the body of believers. Reading the story of God's interaction with His people throughout the ages calls the contemporary reader to see God's work in and through His people today. The Bible calls us to carry one another's burdens and to receive spiritual strength from each other. This love for one another in times of lament sets the table for the final movement of the spiritual formation of reading Scripture.

Loving one another in time of lament will serve as a witness for the world. Otherwise the world will not know we are Jesus' disciples. If we only receive care from "professional" caregivers, then the church has devolved to the level of a community hospital or self-help section of a bookstore. People who lament together model Christ's love and demonstrate God's healing work through Word, Spirit, and fellowship to a world that knows so much suffering. In fact, unless disciples embrace suffering, they have no authority to tell the world about the new life they have in Christ.

Of course, disciples come to the Bible in times other than suffering. In all cases, the Word takes us from the world to relationship with each other in Christ for a witness in the world. The disciple knows the Spirit will help in each of these areas because the Spirit was there when the original writers penned the text.

In the context of spiritual formation, Bible reading should lead disciples to ask three primary questions every time they open the Book:

1. WHAT DID I LEARN?

Individual passages of Scripture exist within the full biblical text. They do not exist as independent words for the day or for private understanding. Each time disciples actively read Scripture they will learn more about God's efforts in reconciling all things to Himself. Actively reading the text will teach or illustrate the need for reconciliation, the constant presence of God's reconciling efforts, the sending of God's people as agents of reconciliation, and believers' faithfulness or unfaithfulness in responding to God's reconciliation offer. Every reading fits within this big picture of the Bible. Reading the text will teach something about God's work in relationship with His creation. When disciples stop with merely understanding, however, they have not really read the Word.

2. HOW CAN I APPLY WHAT I LEARNED?

Understanding leads to action. Discipleship formation of active reading will always lead learners to become doers of the Word. Unfortunately, disciples of every generation face the temptation to just listen to the Word. James called this approach an act of self-deception and an act of forgetfulness. On the other hand, those who become doers of the Word "shall be blessed in his deed." (See James 1:22–25.) If a disciple stops reading without developing some application item, then he or she needs to read again. Reading the same passage multiple times will help disciples live out the text. In cases where the reader does not understand how the text calls for application today, then that person should pray for the Spirit's leading, discuss the text with more mature saints, and consult additional resources as needed.

3. HOW THEN SHOULD I PRAY?

Scripture always calls us beyond our capability. Disciples must have the Spirit's guidance as they read and apply the Word. They will pray about God's redemptive work, the way His people labor together, and how disciples can witness to the world. Moving from understanding to application provides insight into Kingdom-focused praying, as we will see below.

Personal Reflection

Read a unit of Scripture. This might be a paragraph, chapter, or several chapters that relate to a biblical narrative. Use the three framing questions to assist you in actively reading the text.

KINGDOM PRAYING

A recent country song by Jaron Lowenstein and Joel Brentlinger portrays a nominal Christian offering cruel, hateful prayers toward a person (presumably an ex-girl-friend, or something along those lines), prayers such as, "I pray your birthday comes and nobody calls." I think all disciples would agree this kind of prayer would violate Kingdom principles in many ways. On the other hand, prayers that begin from our perception of need also violate Kingdom principles. Prayer must begin with God's purposes rather than our own. In fact, Kingdom praying requires death to self and a new life in Christ. Jesus' model prayer in Matthew 6 provides significant components of this process.

- Jesus taught disciples to pray in relationship with one another. Many people skip over the importance of the first word in the prayer— our. Unless we position ourselves with other members of the body, we will fail to grasp the potential of prayer. God's prayer promises relate to the whole body because prayer always fulfills a missional function.

- Jesus taught the disciples to pray in right relationship with God. Addressing the Father together guarantees we worship and pray appropriately. Failing to acknowledge these relationships can open the door to ungodly praying. If prayer is to the Father, then we stand in the location of sons and daughters. All other relationships convey an emphasis on the prayer rather than on the Father.

- Jesus taught the disciples to pray for the Kingdom to come. The Kingdom must come prior to daily bread or other felt needs. The Kingdom must even come before praying for forgiveness and affirming our active forgiveness of each other. The Kingdom must come before prayer for deliverance from temptation. In short, seeking the Kingdom first in prayer puts all other prayers in their place.

Both Jesus and Paul spoke of the need for our new life in Christ to be established prior to seeking the Kingdom's purposes. Jesus taught Nicodemus that he had to be born again of water and spirit to be able to see the Kingdom (John 3:5). Being born from above remakes our desires and expectations to set the stage for us to rely on the Father's will. Paul told the churches of Rome and Galatia they had a right to cry out "Abba, Father" because of their adoption. Because of this new relationship, disciples have the rights of joint heirs with Christ. While new birth speaks of the total dependence of an infant, adoption speaks of capabilities the Father sees in us. In the Roman world, children were not adopted. In that culture children had little value. Instead, one would adopt an adult with proven experience to carry on the family responsibilities. For example, a number of Roman Caesars adopted the next ruler to make sure someone was in line with the right abilities to lead the empire.

God invites us to join His purposes through Kingdom-focused prayers. We pray because of the gifts and potential the Father has placed in us. To pray solely for our own benefit would be like the Temple priests setting up marketing franchises in the Temple. Jesus still tips over the tables of those who attempt to use Kingdom resources for their own benefit.

Prayer transforms us to seek God's will on earth as in Heaven. The right orientation for prayer forces us to die to self (new birth) and to give up on the old family orientations and habits (adoption) as we approach God together. Unfortunately, the process does not happen without bumps in the road. Paul's prayer guidelines in Romans 8 remind us that anxiety and fear often enable us to cry out "Abba, Father" in Kingdom-shaped ways. In Galatians 4 he spoke to a church that had turned to "weak and beggarly elements" of bondage.

Conducting a prayer review is one critical step in pursuing prayer as spiritual formation rather than "Christmas-list praying." Christmas-list praying simply bombards Heaven with all the things we want to be added to our lives or pains we want to go away. Disciples have the wonderful opportunity to compare their prayer lists with Scripture's teaching. While God does care that we have enough to eat and clothing to wear, praying for these things sounds more like prayers of the world than Kingdom prayers (Matthew 6:32). True disciple prayers take full advantage of the power supply available to see the kingdom of God. All other stuff belongs in the appendix, the fine print at the end of prayers. God knows we have need of these things and will freely add them to us as we pray in line with the Kingdom.

Personal Reflection

Read I Peter 2 and write out two or three prayers that align your petitions with God's eternal Word. Share your prayer requests with a fellow believer.

CONCLUSION

An honest review of our prayers does not always provide an encouraging result. As I look over my daily prayer list and those I hear most Sunday mornings, I see more appendix material, the things God simply wants to add to our lives as we seek His purposes, than I do Kingdom prayers.

Lord, have mercy.

As we saw in the discussion of active reading above, praying naturally flows from the Word. The Word tells the story of God's desire to be with His creation and His initiatives to make this happen. Since He sends His people to be salt, light, and a city on a hill, our Kingdom prayers will pray in the same direction.

Some people wonder why they should pray at all if God knows what we pray for even before we ask. Only by walking closer to Christ can disciples grasp the power of praying in line with God's purpose. Just as Jesus prayed for the Father's will to be done, we too have that privilege. By praying the Word, we can confidently participate in God's purpose—a purpose that will be completed.

Klaus Issler identifies four key divine purposes in our prayer. First, God calls us to prayer to enrich our relationship with Him. Praying God's Word guarantees disciples will develop spiritual maturity. They begin to value and seek the same things that God does. Second, prayer reminds believers to look to God for their sustenance. Prayer, like worship, highlights our dependency on God's providence and ability to supply that which He has promised. By praying the Word, we know the Father will answer our prayer (John 15:7–8). Third, Issler suggests prayer helps believers alleviate their doubts about God. Sadly, James's evaluation holds true for many Christians today: "Ye ask, and receive not, because ye ask amiss, that ye may consume it upon your lusts" (James 4:3). Unanswered prayer can deplete confidence in God. Conversely, prayer in line with God's purposes increases confidence. As we see in James, unanswered prayers flow from personal desires rather than divine purposes as seen in the Word. Finally, prayer prepares disciples to rule and reign with God after the Second Coming. While most Christians believe and look forward to His coming, they forget the reality of our ruling and reigning with Him in the new Heaven and new Earth. While we can be assured that the Marriage Supper will be delightful, eternity will have more purposeful occupations than eating and sharing our stories with one another. Prayer now develops an agreement with God's eternal purposes; such an agreement prepares us to reign with Him (II Timothy 2:12).

As we saw in John 15, Jesus guaranteed disciples would have fruitful prayer lives if they would abide in Him and let the Word exist in them. The end result would be the Father answering the disciples' prayers and the Father being glorified. Any prayer that does not lead to the Father's glory could be classified as abusive use of prayer or stewardship failure.

Scripture contains examples of the apostles' prayers as well as those of their Master. For example, II Thessalonians opens the window on Paul's prayer life. Studying and praying with Paul can effectively transition a novice disciple to a new place in prayer maturity—a place where personal desires or lusts get displaced with Kingdom purposes.

Personal Reflection

1. *Think about the wonder of God's invitation to pray as part of His way to reconcile all of creation to Himself.*
2. *Give thanks for this invitation.*
3. *Add a prayer or two to your Kingdom prayer list as the Spirit speaks to you during this time of thanksgiving.*
4. *Share your growing Kingdom prayers with other disciples. This process strengthens your commitment to pray in line with the Word and Sprit; it also encourages others to grow spiritually.*

PRAYER

Let us pray,

Lord, help us to be overwhelmed by the power of your Word. Forgive us of attempting to conduct our lives in ways that separate us from the power of Your very breath. Just as our mothers and fathers in the faith loved Your Word, we covet a complete dependence on those things which are forever settled. We seek to hear and understand the Word so that we can completely surrender to it. Though we will never understand all You have spoken through the biblical authors, we can pursue that which we do understand today. Teach us to pray in line with that understanding. We pledge to use the power of prayer for Kingdom purposes rather than our own pleasure and security—we have placed those two longings in the authority of the Word.

In Jesus' name,

Amen

6 | *Fasting and Service*

Many people in Jesus' day took the one annual day of fasting from Moses' Law—the Day of Atonement—and decided two days each week, Monday and Thursday, should be set as fast days for pious people. People just kept adding fast days, but they saw little results from doing more. Some people in our day teach that fasting is something we can do in order to get God's attention. If the Cross, empty tomb, and Pentecost's upper room do not guarantee we already have God's attention, then no amount of fasting could ever tear God away from what keeps Him preoccupied. As we have mentioned at other points in this book, *spiritual formation is the lifelong personal and communal commitment to know Christ, to be remade in His image as a part of new creation, and to be on His mission.*

Jesus spent more time telling His followers how not to fast than to give directions for doing so. Outside of His miraculous forty-day fast recorded in Matthew 4, we do not see Jesus or the disciples engaging in fasting as we see them engage in other aspects of spiritual formation.

In Acts we also see limited fasting. As seekers, Saul and Cornelius fasted in pursuit of God's purposes. Prophets and teachers in Antioch seem to have had a practice of praying and fasting; on one of those occasions the Spirit called for a new missionary strategy. They fasted and prayed some more before ordaining the first two missionary candidates and sending them on their way. Finally Paul and Barnabas used the fasting/ordaining pattern as they ordained elders in various churches.

Paul does not give principles for fasting as he does for prayer. While prayer can be found in most of his writings, fasting is found only in I Corinthians 7:5 where the emphasis is on limiting marital sexual abstinence to agreed-upon times of prayer. Paul calls the church to "pray without ceasing" (I Thessalonians 5:17), but he does not give directions for fasting. The New Testament church seemed to make fasting a matter of Christian freedom rather than a standardized practice for spiritual formation.

Personal Reflection

Why do you think the Pharisees' fasting produced little to no results? What are some ways their fasting produced negative results?

THE CHALLENGE

When asked about the lack of fasting in Jesus' practice and teaching curriculum, the Teacher responded by asking a question and telling a couple of parables. All three of His responses pointed to the new age that changed practices from the past. The Pharisees and disciples of John represented two forms of asceticism that highly valued the fasting tradition. Jesus told His questioners the students did not fast because the Bridegroom's presence meant this was party time. In fact Mark places this story following a confrontation over Jesus' preferences for parties. He not only ate with publicans and sinners, He also chose one of them for His inner circle. His disciples did not fast because the pending wedding changed everything.

The twin parables also underscored the radical changes taking place. In Mark 2 Jesus does not rebuke fasting practices of Pharisees or John's followers. Rather than rebuking others, He stated they both belonged to an age now passed. They were the old cloth and old wineskin. Jesus' presence brought new cloth and fresh, still-fermenting wine. To fast like they did would be like making the hole in an old cloth even worse and ruining what little value the old, nonpliable skins possessed. At least the skins could carry water if they could not handle the new wine.

Fasting presents a challenge for spiritual formation as do a number of other disciplines. Practice does not always make perfect as music and math teachers often remind us. Using poor musical or math techniques only reinforces poor behaviors. Unless spiritual disciplines follow the new day brought on by the Bridegroom, new cloth, and fresh wine, they will de-form rather than re-form us. Examining some de-forming aspects of fasting can help us prepare for new cloth and new skins.

In Matthew 6 Jesus discussed three key elements of Jewish piety: prayer, alms giving, and fasting. In each case He suggested practitioners can easily reduce the discipline to a hypocritical farce. Rather than acting on motivations that come from a right relationship with God, the practices happen to gain acclaim before others. Praying, giving, and fasting with the hope of being noticed de-forms believers by perpetuating self-centered narcissism. Getting a trophy for praying or paying means the person got the reward they sought—the reward of humanity.

Fasting falls within the same potential trap. The Old Testament law only mandated fasting on the Day of Atonement. On that day everyone fasted as a sign of repentance. As with other grief moments in antiquity, people would often change out of better garments and wear coarse garments. They would refrain from normal face washing and anointing with oil. In the "new wine" period Jesus changed the paradigm. Now folks *should* wear their normal clothes and take care to wash their face and go about normal routines while fasting. Jesus did not give reasons or contexts for fasting; He only explained the mechanics of fasting.

The Old Testament prophets used similar language as they rebuked their audience in an effort to lead them closer to God. Isaiah 58 gives one such example. The prophet began with a description that makes us think all is going well. Who would not want this assessment for their local church assembly? "Yet they seek me daily, and delight to know my ways, as a nation that did righteousness, and forsook not the ordinance of their God: they ask of me the ordinances of justice; they take delight in approaching to God" (Isaiah 58:2).

Notice the strong actions the prophet used in defining Israel's spiritual state. If fasting produces this kind of practice, then we need to recover their model. Sadly, what appeared to be spiritual actually stank of self-centered carnality.

The Lord rebelled against their fasting. They sought pleasure, created division, took advantage of others, and engaged in harmful debate. He no longer wanted to even hear their voices. Israel's God demanded His people replace their soul affliction, bowed heads, and sackcloth and ashes with acts of care and kindness for others. God wanted them to understand that when others suffer, they themselves suffer.

Jesus and Isaiah challenge us today. Western Christianity often serves self-centered ends. How often have you heard people say they really did not get much out of worship in a Sunday service or they need to change churches because the larger one across town has more to offer their family? Would a prayer review reveal self-centered needs or Kingdom-focused concern for those in difficulty? When we pray for God's blessings exclusively on our own country, rather than for the blessings of the world, then have we misused Kingdom authority? We stand in danger of hearing the Lord say, "Stop praying!" as He did for Israel on multiple occasions. Spiritual disciplines that seek to enrich or edify self, either by getting attention from others or misusing Kingdom power for one's own pleasure, serve to de-form us rather than form us.

Personal Reflection

1. *How did the Day of Atonement fasting differ from later fasting done by the Pharisees?*

2. *Jesus examined prayer, almsgiving, and fasting in the context of new Kingdom living. Why do you think He selected these three behaviors? How can His selection and Kingdom application guide you in your spiritual formation?*

THE LORD'S FAST

The Lord's fast intercedes and acts on behalf of others. Jesus' own fast in Matthew 4 related to His ordination just like those in Acts 13 (missionaries) and Acts 14 (elders). The Spirit led Him into the wilderness for a period of testing. Jesus demonstrated He would not use His authority for self-gratification even in time of need (turning stones to bread), miraculous signs to draw attention to His own miracle campaign (jumping off the Temple into angels' hands), or to abandon the painful journey before Him (false worship to gain dominion). Jesus then began His public ministry.

As illustrated above, the Lord used Isaiah to call His people to a similar fast in Isaiah 58. This kind of fast required the people to recognize the blessings and power they did have rather than clamor for more. Fasting set them free from pursuing their own purposes as they shared God's blessings with those in need. They should undo the heavy burdens, release the oppressed, break yokes, feed the hungry, bring the poor into their houses, and clothe the naked.

Notice the spiritual formation that happens with the Lord's fast. The Lord promised open communication, light in the night moments, and water in their desert land. Revival would take place. Israel had the chance to receive a new name, The Repairer of the Breaches, because of their ability to rebuild all the treasured places.

By turning from their own needs and using their own resources to alleviate the suffering of others, they received the most precious of rewards. The spiritual discipline of abstaining from one's own pleasures for the gifting of others radically transforms us into the image of the One who calls us.

Personal Reflection

1. *In three sentences or less, describe Jesus' personal use of fasting.*

2. *Examine your last period of fasting. Compare your purpose to Jesus' purposes.*

GRACEFUL SERVICE

The Lord's fast can be our reality because of the many waves of grace that crash over us. "And of his fulness have all we received, and grace for grace. For the law was given by Moses, but grace and truth came by Jesus Christ" (John 1:16–17). Discipleship calls us to live graciously in our world. While the Law consisted of graciousness in its own right, grace had to dwell and die among us to change us. Only in Christ could God reconcile the world unto Himself. In doing so God has transmitted the opportunity and authority to do works of reconciliation and speak words of reconciliation to our world. In fact, we live as ambassadors for Christ. (See II Corinthians 5:17–20.)

The Lord's fast maximizes the benefits of being this new creature in Christ. This fast helps us take our eyes off ourselves and gives us vision to see the possibilities of transformation in the world. Then we do something about it. While we must first see the needs of the world, fasting helps us move beyond the "be warmed and filled" stage James warns us about. All our relationships, from intimate ones of our own house to the enemy who plots evil against us, become opportunities for grace to flow.

The Lord's fast as spiritual formation enables us to take inventory of our gifts and blessings as Kingdom resources.

As we will see in chapter 9, we live as stewards of these gifts. If we receive freely, then we will be able to give freely. Sociologists might call this process the accumulation of social capital. Because the disciples were committed to live in accordance with Kingdom principles, they generated resources to care for others. Of course, we understand this process happens as a function of spiritual empowerment from above, but the principle holds true. As we participate in the Lord's fast, we shift from being a consumption driven people to a spiritually productive people. We utilize Kingdom gifts on behalf of others rather than for ourselves.

The Spirit may call us to fast when we find ourselves seeking our own pleasure and blessings rather than the needs of others. As we saw in Isaiah 58 and Matthew 4, this kind of fast places God's purposes for others at the center of everything we do. If we fail in this transition from our own prerogatives to following God's revealed mission, then we place ourselves in grave danger of losing spiritual authority.

Personal Reflection

What steps might we take individually and corporately to move from fasting for our spiritual growth objectives or specific cares to noting our resources, seeing needs in the world, and finding appropriate ways to share our blessings?

A Biblical Case Study

Perhaps a case study of the first generation of disciples might help us see the consequences of missing this shift. Mark 9 records two fascinating settings. The first narrative tells the story of the Transfiguration. Jesus took three disciples with Him to prepare for the next leg of the journey in much the same way He would later do in the Gethsemane Garden prayer meeting. The Transfiguration helped Jesus prepare for His upcoming death: His clothes became white as snow, He had a conference with Moses and Elijah, and they all heard words of divine confirmation as had happened at Jesus' baptism. The disciples were fearful and asked one another what "the rising from the dead should mean" (Mark 9:10).

Meanwhile the valley narrative examines a separate but parallel story. The remaining nine disciples continued with their Teacher's business in His absence. Surrounding communities knew that Jesus and His pupils demonstrated an uncanny ability to cast out demons. They succeeded at exorcising evil spirits when other professional exorcists failed. From Mark 6:7–13 we know Jesus had already given His students spiritual authority to cast out demons. Their successful exercise of this authority became common knowledge. The troubled father brought his demon-possessed son to the disciples. He fully expected them to cast out the demons just as easily as Jesus would.

The nine disciples tried and failed.

Something robbed them of the spiritual authority they had possessed in the past. Jesus castigated them for being part of a faithless generation. The demons could only be cast out by prayer. The biblical text forces us to ask what happened between successful use of spiritual authority in Mark 6 and unbelief in Mark 9?

Disciples today experience similar challenges faced by those original disciples. When the Teacher chooses us to follow Him and fills us with His Spirit, we celebrate the wonder of being a new creation in Him. Faith soars. Prayers explode. Miracles happen. Worship thrives. Then the journey takes an unexpected turn. Faith suffers. Prayers wane. Miracles dwindle. Worship quietens. Our own story reflects a condition where spiritual authority diminishes in its effectiveness.

The original disciple class learned two lessons in Mark 8. The first, the confession that Jesus was the Christ, brought tremendous insight and strength. Perhaps that moment contained more wonder and awe than millennia of sunsets and a thousand initial breaths of a whole world's generation of babies. The second revelation, that Christ would suffer rejection and death before being raised again, brought confusion. Peter went from hearing heavenly revelation to being labeled Satan. They could accept the truth of Jesus' identity, but they rejected the plan that followed that revelation. What a rapid status change! Not only would Jesus die, they too would have to take up their own cross and follow Him. This second call brought doubt.

New revelation calls for new responsibility. Carrying that new responsibility requires spiritual formation, or authority will be lost. The disciples went from casting out devils to failing in their mission. The needy crowds could not tell from their point of view, but anguishing fathers quickly learned the students could no longer perform the works of their Teacher.

This kind of work only comes by prayer.

The disciples needed to pray to accept God's missional plan. Until then, those with the greatest need would suffer.

Mark 9 includes even more evidence of the students' unwillingness to grasp the Teacher's plan. The first symptom emerges in verses 33–37. Instead of accepting the suffering, cross-shaped path, the student council meeting filled with debate over who among them was the greatest. If their Teacher was the Christ, then they should be in line for honorable positions also. They had a chance to get on the ground floor of the first global business conglomerate. Jesus went into Teacher mode. He used both direct instruction and an enacted metaphor. They must become servants of all. They must stoop to the insignificance of a child so that the world would receive them as children of the name.

The second symptom emerges in verse 38–41. Being a pupil of the Teacher must have felt like being an upperclassman at a prestigious university. For some reason Harvard or Cambridge University students feel a little different about their educational experiences than those of us who attend a shopping strip outlet of the local community college. The founding student body of disciples felt the same way. They saw some other man casting out devils in Jesus' name and told him to cut it out. Not only were they not following Jesus, they complained, but "he followed not us." Perhaps failed spiritual exercises stung even more when outsiders did not suffer a similar setback. While this passage raises other critical issues, we certainly must grasp the call to humility.

The Lord's fast and this kind of prayer call us to lay down our own prerogatives. Amazingly, the apostle Paul believed we could follow Christ closely enough to have this mind of humility. (See Philippians 2.)

The story does not end here. After being filled with the Spirit, the disciples lived on behalf of others. When their crosses brought threats of additional suffering in Acts 4, the disciples prayed for boldness on the mission rather than alleviation of their own suffering. Now they knew how to pray like Jesus did.

Personal Reflection

1. *Consider spiritual growth points in the past. Identify revelation that preceded your growth.*

2. *Consider spiritually trying times in the past. Identify revelations that you avoided or misunderstood at the time.*

3. *Think about the sermons, Bible studies, words of knowledge, or prophecy you heard over the last two weeks. What was the Spirit trying to show you? How have you responded in changed thinking, emotions, or actions? What prayers do you need to pray to come further in line with the Spirit's leading? How does your learning and application free you to serve others?*

CONCLUSION

Jesus forms His disciples in His image. Being like Him requires serving like Him. Serving like Him requires parallel spiritual disciplines in fasting and prayer to put others at the center of mission rather than ourselves.

Speaking from the experience of one who has celebrated fifty spiritual birthdays and thirty-eight years of being a credentialed minister, I must confess the journey has not followed anything like I thought it would be. I do not think I wrestle with these realities alone. When the path takes turns, becomes too steep, or gets lost in the fog of confusion, we need to spend additional time in prayer and fasting to retain spiritual authority. That spiritual authority comes from walking in both the revelation of truth and acceptance of the Teacher's wisdom in setting the course. Rather than seeking exile from difficult times, spiritual formation calls us to carry our cross and pray for ways to serve others during those times.

- Sometimes ministry goes so slowly, so we look for other things to do while we wait for God to do His thing.

- Sometimes we trust our own ability and resources when God does not seem to follow through on His promises.

- Sometimes the dream literally crashes around us, so we abandon hope that we can hear God's voice and that we have a purpose.

- Sometimes others radically misunderstand our calling, so we try to prove we are right, or we do nothing until all the doors swing open with the respect we think we deserve.

- Sometimes we try and fail—repeatedly—so we lose the focus to try again. Instead we grow content with "just being saved." We trust the truth of Jesus, but we no longer trust His faithfulness in our own lives.

- Sometimes others do not do their part, so we either quit our work until others get busy or face burnout by shouldering both their and our responsibilities.

- Sometimes the world changes so quickly that we do not know what to do. We lose confidence that the Lord can help us to bridge the gap between the gospel and a pagan world.

- Sometimes we do not see a model for us to follow in ministry when Jesus calls us to some new missional challenge, so we do not take the risk to pioneer a new kind of ministry.

All these possibilities represent a single threat to our faith—not believing God knows what He is doing. Failing to accept new revelation reduces faith, diminishes spiritual authority, and misuses our energy on meeting our own needs. In these moments the Lord's fast can show us when to repent of rejecting God's plan, renew our vision for those around us, and revitalize our service for God on behalf of others. The Lord's fast restores spiritual authority.

Personal Reflection

1. *Review your key points of learning from this chapter and responses to discussion questions.*

2. *Plan your next fast. Share your plan with a spiritual friend who can help you focus your prayer on the Lord's fast.*

PRAYER

I pray the wonder of God's truth and trust in His plan take ever deeper roots in your spirit. I pray you walk in the possibilities before you in this season of your life. I pray your prayer and fasting enables you to transition through the quest for your own healing and answers to your questions to a celebration of the magnitude of blessings in your life. I pray you follow the Spirit's direction to serve those in need. I pray your mind thinks like a reconciling ambassador. I pray your heart experiences the fullness of joy and hope in being a peacemaker in the world. I pray your hands actively feed the hungry, comfort the sick, and shelter the wounded. I pray your testimony causes others to experience new birth for themselves.

In Jesus' name,

Amen

7 | Thanksgiving and Blessing

During this season of my life, I deeply cherish conversations with my parents. Family gatherings invariably include stories of the past. We do not argue over which day of the week something happened, the color of toy cars from Grandma Tucker back in the 1960s or who did what first. Instead the stories convey who we were, are, and will be as a family. As a child, I had five grandmothers and three grandfathers; my oldest daughter attended my college graduation along with my mother, grandmother, and great-grandmother. While my grandparents have all gone to eternity, they remain in our memories, stories, and even our outlook on life. Our stories make us different from other families.

Being in Christ makes us a new family. As such we carry the responsibility of doing the Father's will. (See Matthew 12:47–50.) We experience new birth and adoption. Stories of the past take on new meaning and purpose. Our walk, talk, and perspective of the future carry the distinctive touches of our new creatureliness. We gratefully accept the opportunity to be holy as our Father is holy. This holiness permeates every aspect of our lives. We embrace the wonder of being a separate and identifiable people, a people God chooses to be what

Goheen calls a contrast people. Throughout history God has always had a people who could be easily identified as being separate. Our separateness attracts others to the wonder of relationship with the Creator. He is restoring all things to Himself. The Bible serves as a record of the chosen people's faithfulness to and deviance from God's gracious call.

Some marks of separation seem arbitrary while others could be found in neighboring cultures. Not plowing with an ox and a mule or wearing blended fibers might be irrelevant to outsiders, but God used these codes and others to form ex-slaves into His chosen people. All people groups of that era had similar behavioral and eating taboos. Worshiping only one God and practicing circumcision, however, made Israel radically different from its neighbors. As modern believers, we also have external markers that differentiate us from our neighbors: gender distinction, modesty, and abstinence from mood-altering substances such as illicit drugs and alcohol. In a pluralist society such as ours, insistence on the uniqueness of Jesus separates us as well.

In this chapter we will explore spiritual disciplines related to another critical area of holiness—holiness of our emotions. Much of the world suffers from a loss of hope and joy. An exploration of the New Testament demonstrates Jesus and the apostles provide significant guidance on emotional holiness because they lived in a dark, dangerous, and uncertain world just as we do. For example, Jesus' audience would not have thought His story about a mugging in broad daylight was strange at all; instead they found the Samaritan's neighborly example to be incredulous.

THANK-FILLED LIVING

The New Testament contains stories of thankful people, commands to be thankful, and critiques of being unthankful. Jesus found the fact that only one leper returned to give God glory a remarkable event. (See Luke 17:12–20.) Paul prescribed thankfulness in the context of the peace of God and unity of the body (Colossians 3:15). The same apostle identified the neglect of glorifying God and unthankfulness as the beginning of the downward spiral that led to foolishness, idolatry, lust, and changing the truth of God into a lie. (See Romans 1:21–26.)

Followers of Christ must practice the discipline of thankfulness—in everything. In fact Paul identifies this discipline as central to the will of God (I Thessalonians 5:18). Thanksgiving cannot be relegated to one holiday each year. Practicing the discipline of thanksgiving separates us from our neighbors. While parents teach their children to say thanks when a grandparent or friend gives them something, they often do not model an attitude of thankfulness in their own lives. Our responses to unfortunate events and difficult situations in the workplace may be instructive. We often think about what we deserve, our rights, and finding someone to blame. We tend to experience emotional turmoil when we feel disrespected, devalued, and overlooked. An orientation toward self or one's own group marks a people as unholy. While disciples may be disrespected or devalued, they learn to focus on God's unending stream of blessings as a way to live thank-filled lives.

As with many spiritual disciplines, repentance must be our first step in the process. A repentant posture enables us to identify unholy attitudes, practices, and beliefs. For example, Western culture's valuing of the individual has an unintended consequence of a sense of entitlement. An entitlement focus magnifies the stuff we have as stuff we deserve. Entitlement produces ever-expanding expectations of what belongs to me or to us. Once we expect things because of who we are, what we have done, or our position, we have poisoned the soil against thanksgiving. Discipleship calls us to repent of entitlement and other sources of unthankfulness.

A second step in thanksgiving's school consists of observation. In our global wage economy we find ourselves greatly distanced from those who gift us with so many blessings. A swipe of the credit card buys a loaf of bread. We do not give thanks for the bread; we earned it. Think for a moment of the thousands of hands needed to get that loaf of bread to the store shelf. We immediately think of farmers and bakers. Closer observation illuminates the contributions of miners and steel works that provide the raw material for tractors, plows, ovens, trucks, and store shelves. Oil-well roughnecks, engineers, refinery workers, hydroelectric dam operators, and cashiers provide fuel for all parts of the system. In many cases, wives and mothers cooked meals for those workers. Weavers spun thread and made material to be cut and sown by seamstresses. The list of contributors to our loaf of bread is endless, yet we hold to a hollow myth of independence as a way to distance our lives from so many people who share their resources with us. Ultimately, of course, we realize every good gift comes from above (James 1:17).

We could also open our eyes to the way God gifts us spiritually through others in the body of believers. Each disciple's life receives from endless streams of spiritual gifts from the local as well as global church. If a human body has roughly sixty thousand miles of arteries, veins, and capillaries to distribute one million barrels of blood, enough to fill three super tankers, in a lifetime, how much more complex and wonderful are the interconnections in the body of Christ? Each part supplies the needs of other parts of the body, and in return it receives the gifts from other members.

One sign of Jesus' miracle ministry is related to the opening of blind eyes. Perhaps praying for our eyes to be open to the many blessings we receive each day would provide evidence that we are a contrast people. Acknowledging all the blessings in our lives serves to retune our hearts. Holy hearts value the gifts of breath, water, moving of the Spirit, and warmth of a friend's touch. Holy hearts also freely give of themselves as contributions to the well-being of others. Holy people celebrate the miracle of God's reconciliation in the world. Rather than complaining about racism, hatred, and inequity, holy hearts acknowledge the unmerited gifts they receive and prepare themselves to gift both the victims and perpetrators of violence. Holy hearts have no other option—they stand in a long stream of blessings.

Finally, they go beyond standing in the stream of blessings to expressing the wonder of cherished simple gifts. They thank the Father above for every gift they see and in anticipation for those they will discover. They thank friends and family for shared joy and love. They even thank their neighbors, both next door and around the world, for their shared treasures. Finally, they thankfully contribute their own work, love, prayer, encouragement, and creativity to the good of others.

What a wonderful opportunity for disciples to witness to our world today! That kind of thankful witness could not be hid under a bushel.

Persnal Reflection

Spiritual formation calls us to evaluate our current state of spiritual growth. Evaluating our thankfulness is one such assessment.

1. *Give an example of thankfulness from the last week or two.*

2. *Give an example of unthankfulness or lack of gratitude.*

   a. *What contributed to the lack of thankfulness?*

   b. *How is the Spirit calling you to repent?*

   c. *Examine all the people and systems that have contributed to your life in this season of ungratefulness. How has God gifted you through those many streams of blessings?*

3. *Write a letter, make a phone call, or ask someone to share a meal to convey your deep gratitude for his or her gifts in your life.*

THE CALL TO BLESS

One does not need to earn a PhD in clinical psychology to know that hurt people hurt others. Every day of our lives we experience the reality of this truth. From the neighborhood playground to the corporate boardroom, those who do not find healing for the wounds in their lives will live both to defend themselves and to perpetuate the shame and hurt heaped on them. The cycle of blame began with our first parents in the Garden and continues to this day.

A review of Scripture reveals the vital emotional spiritual discipline of blessing others. What naturally happened in a patriarch's final days of life should be our daily experience. The patriarchs blessed their children before dying. Perhaps one of the most moving examples can be found in the closing chapters of Job. Job knew suffering on all levels. His body screamed in agony. He suffered abandonment and shame at the hands of others. His spirit cried for answers to the injustice of his children's death, loss of wealth and status, and confusion over his inability to make sense of what happened.

As Job received healing, he blessed his friends in prayer. Decades later he blessed his second group of children, his last seven sons and three daughters. His suffering and subsequent healing prepared him to bless all his children. Even a casual reading of Job 42 points out the difference between his blessings and those of Jacob or David. It is likely Jacob had more than the one daughter who lived in the vortex of so much suffering and bloodshed, but those daughters received no mention. For one of David's princesses to gain a place in Scripture she had to suffer at the hands of a brother, see the brother die, and witness the consequences of a civil war. Job blessed differently. His experience of shame and powerlessness caused him to bless his sons and his daughters. In fact, Scripture only records Job's daughters' names. Jemima, Kezia, and Keren-happuch received inheritances along with their brothers. While other girls lived as chattel to be passed from father to husband to son, these girls knew the wonder of a father's blessings. Job's blessings went far beyond cultural norms.

Numbers 6 records the Lord's command for Moses to instruct Aaron and the next generation of priests in the art of blessing others. "The Lord bless thee, and keep thee: The Lord make his face shine upon thee, and be gracious unto thee: The Lord lift up his countenance upon thee, and give thee peace. And they shall put my name upon the children of Israel and I will bless them" (Numbers 6:24–27).

The Lord's name rested on Israel by delivering them from Egypt, taking them through the desert experiences, giving them a Promised Land and purpose, and placing His name on the chosen city. He blessed them with Sabbath, food, and divine protection. He blessed them with children. In this passage, however, we see the Lord's sovereign choice in placing His name on the generations to come by the priestly blessing.

As New Testament believers we understand the name of Jesus being placed on us in baptism. We know the wonder of remission of sin and becoming new creatures as we live out the baptized life. While baptism happens only one time in a person's life, the placing of Christ's name should be a reoccurring event. God blesses disciples to such an extent that they can bless others; they can even bless, serve, and pray for those who despitefully use them. Blessing others flows from and demonstrates the disciples' identity as children of God. (See Matthew 5:44–45.)

Sadly, many people live their lives trying to prove they are worthy of blessings. Even when an abusive or distant parent dies, many sons and daughters continue to walk as "unblessed" children. Consequently, they fail in blessing others. The spiritual discipline of blessing flows from the discipline of thanksgiving. Aaron and his sons could bless others because they were blessed. Disciples bless others because they live blessed lives. As they celebrate blessings in their own lives, they look for ways to bless others. Disciples do not evaluate a prospective person's worth of blessings. Instead they seek opportunities to bless because they themselves have experienced undeserved blessings.

Jesus chose to bless the "under-blessed" segments of society. He placed children on His knee in a time when children had little value. He had to go through Samaria to bless a much disregarded lady at the well. He befriended and blessed lepers, prostitutes, and tax collectors. Perhaps we could even call Jesus a blessing machine.

Disciples will need to intentionally focus on blessing others during certain periods of their lives. Placing a focus on the discipline of blessing habituates the process to where disciples automatically dispense blessings wherever they go. Blessing others transitions from a discipline to an honored opportunity, as natural to daily living as drinking water. Getting to the natural state of blessing, however, will take intentional efforts. A pastor friend of mine in Texas celebrates the joy of blessing others by intentionally looking for someone to bless each day. I can witness to the healing power of such a life since I have crossed his path of blessing on multiple occasions. He joyfully smiles as he blesses. One shares in the ultimate blesser's gifts in that pastor's life as he shares a smile, a handshake, a story, a ministry experience, and even a gift that symbolizes the blessing.

Personal Reflection

1. *Reflect on those who have blessed you recently. How did they place you in the stream of blessings they had received from God? What words or actions did they use to bless you?*

2. *Make a list of ten people you can bless. Identify two specific ways you can bless each person. Begin to implement your plan within a few days.*

EMOTIONAL HOLINESS

The priestly blessing promised the inclusion of peace, perhaps the most unfulfilled of human quests. We certainly live in a world that finds little return on its peace investment. According to the *Washington Post* the US global defense spending in 2016 was about $597 billion of the world's total defense spending of $1.58 trillion. In spite of the tremendous investment in defense and peace, the world knows little peace. As a result of global conflicts, the world now has about sixty million displaced persons. Even these startling figures do not capture the degree of hopelessness, fear, and anxiety in the world today. Regardless of one's political leanings, the 2016 US election cycle seemed to fan the flames of emotional turmoil.

Fear results from incidences of crime and other forms of loss as well as from a media-saturated world. We are inundated with news selected by the old adage, "what bleeds leads." Followers of Christ, however, receive both the promise of peace and the command not to live in fear. "Peace I leave with you, my peace I give unto you: not as the world giveth, give I unto you. Let not your heart be troubled, neither let it be afraid" (John 14:27). Following the Prince of Peace requires spiritual disciplines that lead to emotional holiness. Following Jesus links keeping His commandments to loving Him and being a recipient of His love. Obedient lovers of Christ will receive the blessing of being the very abode of that Prince of Peace. Conversely, lack of obedient discipleship inhibits this abiding, transformative relationship.

As we have seen in chapter 2, abiding in Christ produces the fruit of joyfulness. In the New Testament, joy accompanied the angelic announcement of Christ's birth and the wise men's observation of His star. Those who do not really understand Jesus' means of bringing about emotional holiness will usually look for joy "in the sweet by and by." We see this in the crowd's Palm Sunday accolades. They could rejoice in what God was doing in Christ. They believed Jesus because of all the mighty acts He did. They even blessed Him as "the king that cometh in the name of the Lord." Unfortunately, they could not conceive of a situation where Jesus would actually bring "peace on earth" as proclaimed by the angels at Jesus' birth. They believed peace resided in Heaven, far beyond their reach. The Palm Sunday crowd's excarnational hope for peace prevented them from living through the coming crises. Professed words of faith usually encounter a trial to determine whether the profession has significant roots. The crowds who could not see peace in their chaotic world quickly changed from blessing the Lord to calling for His crucifixion.

Without emotional holiness, disciples will also falter in times of crises because circumstances determine their feelings and perspectives. In itself, this outcome robs potential disciples of abundant life; however, the crises go far deeper, as we see in I Thessalonians 1:5–7: "For our gospel came not unto you in word only, but also in power, and in the Holy Ghost, and in much assurance; as ye know what manner of men we were among you for your sake. And ye became followers of us, and of the Lord, having received the word in much affliction, with joy of the Holy Ghost: So that ye were ensamples to all that believe in Macedonia and Achaia."

Paul and his ministry team modeled the gospel in word, power, and assurance in the Holy Spirit. Incarnational holiness transformed the new believers as they followed Jesus. Their afflictions did not determine their emotional state; the Holy Spirit did.

Personal Reflection

1. *As with all holiness, emotional holiness comes from God rather than from within the disciple. Identify one or two areas of emotional distress that you either currently experience or experienced in the last six months. What triggered those emotional responses?*

2. *How might you look to Christ as the source of emotional strength? You might consider the role of worship, prayer, meditation on the Word, and serving others as possible actions to bring further holiness focus to your emotions.*

HOPEFUL LIVING

Incarnational discipleship enables saints to live in accordance with the three eternal principles: faith, hope, and love. Perhaps in Pentecostal celebration of the new birth experience, many believers seek to follow the ways of love and faith. Love naturally rises to the surface as we see the impact of God's choice in loving the world to the extent that He sent His only begotten son (John 3:16). The greatest commandment has the twin expressions of loving God and loving one's neighbor as one's self (Luke 10:27–28). Finally, love for one another serves as a witness to the world that we are Jesus' disciples (John 13:34–35). Since faith justifies us (Romans 3:28), makes us pleasing in the sight of God (Hebrews 11:6), and provides guidance for our daily walk (II Corinthians 5:7), we must mature from the small measure of faith to a life characterized by a breastplate of faith coupled with love as seen in I Thessalonians 5:8.

Incarnational discipleship cultivates hope along with faith and love. While faith, the content of the gospel, and complete trust in Christ defeat fear, hope vanquishes despair. Hope lives in the real world rather than abiding in some optimism that everything will work out somehow. Hope stands in the broken and dark reality of this world while placing complete confidence that Jesus will bring to pass that which He said He would do. Hope, however, goes a step further than a faith statement—hope enables disciples to act like the end is already complete. One might say hope is faith lived out in real time.

In everyday language, hope seems more like a wish. Folks will hope for good weather on the weekend or for a raise this year. They have no evidence for the wish. They also cannot act on the wish as if it has already come to pass.

Hope can and should be lived out in personal, family, and church life. Faith lets us know that all suffering will be gone in the end because Scripture tells us so. Hope takes this belief and puts it to work now. Rather than living in despair when life brings pain, loss of a home, or death of a loved one, incarnational discipleship lives in persistent hope that the present reality will fade into the eternal blessing that is already settled.

Spiritual disciplines related to emotional holiness call disciples to examine their state of daily hopefulness. When this hope temporarily fades from a disciple, then they must rediscover the love of God and power of the Holy Spirit. In some ways, hope serves as one of the lasting markers of the evidence of the Holy Spirit in our lives. Paul puts this well in Romans 5:5: "And hope maketh not ashamed; because the love of God is shed abroad in our hearts by the Holy Ghost which is given unto us." While disciples will experience challenges that come from associating with Christ and the fellowship of His suffering, they do not lose hope. Hope suspends the natural human response of despair in favor of life in the Spirit.

Immature prayer lives can lead us away from hopeful living. If we have hope because we believe prayer will deliver us from moments of suffering now, then we may experience extended periods of despair. Some Christians see suffering as the absence of God's presence, failure of God's plan, departure from the will of God, or an obstacle to the Christian walk. Perhaps they even see suffering as a barrier to witness in a world bent on exercising the human right to pursue happiness above all else. James and Peter offer an alternative perspective. James 1:2 calls us to count it all joy when trials come our way. Peter echoes a similar perspective when he calls us to joyfully anticipate fiery trials rather than thinking their occurrences are some strange imposition in our lives. Peter calls us to live out a life of emotional holiness: to rejoice now in suffering with Christ and rejoicing later when His glory is revealed (I Peter 4:12–13).

Walking in emotional holiness requires developing a discipline of examining and living in accordance with Jesus' own experience. Perhaps Hebrews 12:2–3 puts it best: "Looking unto Jesus the author and finisher of our faith; who for the joy that was set before him endured the cross, despising the shame, and is set down at the right hand of the throne of God. For consider him that endured such contradiction of sinners against himself, lest ye be wearied and faint in your minds."

Jesus turned the tables on shame. The suffering should have brought shame and despair, but Jesus acted on what was already accomplished before Him. Fearfulness and weariness of mind call us to look again to the author and finisher of our faith. Instead of failing in our emotions, we will see the big, completed picture. Such a renewed vision enables us to start living the consequences of eternity now. What a wonderful opportunity!

Personal Reflection

1. *Define biblical hope. How does our culture's use of hope differ from a biblical perspective?*

2. *Examine the evidence of hopelessness around you. How would society's "hope quotient" change if everyone knew Jesus' kingdom is coming—a time when all suffering will be gone*

and all the saved will enjoy God's direct presence (I John 3)?

3. *Prayerfully consider your own hope status at this time. Do you feel like you are growing in Kingdom-oriented hope or still suffering from emotions controlled by today's reality? How might you begin to live more hopefully today in light of the finished Kingdom?*

FELLOWSHIP AND JOY

Examining emotional holiness reminds us that seeking hope or joy alone is futile. Emotional holiness requires life in community. In the Creation narratives, God conveyed the truth of fellowship's humanizing power. By himself, Adam was not good, according to the Creator's evaluation. Adam did not reflect the image of God in a well-rounded way when he was alone. With fellowship, however, Adam became more human; together they became very good. The early church followed in Jesus' discipleship principle of fellowship also. The Twelve had shared much of their lives while walking through the initial stages of becoming disciples; the newly Spirit-filled believers would do the same, as we see in Acts 2:42–47. In fact, praising God in fellowship led to favor with the people and set the stage for the Lord to add to the church.

Shared mission and prayer produce joy by looking beyond the present circumstances. For example, Paul implored the Roman church to join with him in prayer. (See Romans 15:30–32.) "Striving prayer" certainly went beyond an occasional mention. The apostle underscored the urgency by anchoring the request to "the Lord Jesus

Christ's sake, and for the love of the Spirit." The specifics of Paul's request included: (1) deliverance from unbelievers, (2) success in taking the missionary offering from the "field" to the mother church in Jerusalem, and (3) the much anticipated time together in Rome. By sharing in prayer, they would be joyfully united and refreshed in the Spirit.

Paul found joy in fellowship with individual disciples as well. He never stopped praying for Timothy, his son in the gospel. Somehow the elder had heard of difficulty that had brought Timothy to tears. Prayer, unity of the Spirit, and anticipated fellowship brought the possibility of renewed joy for both. Paul did not stop with prayer—he worked to encourage the younger man by highlighting spiritual heritage, enumeration of spiritual gifts, underscoring shared holy calling, and personal experiences of suffering. In fact, Paul spoke of his own trials and abandonment while in prison. The elder's words helped to explain how he stayed emotionally balanced rather than suffering shame. He encouraged the younger man to "hold fast" as well.

The Philippian letter emphasizes this fellowship context of joy for groups of individuals and the church at large. Paul remained hopeful his work had not been in vain. Rather than being discouraged, as one might anticipate, his "sacrifice and service" brought joy on his and the church's behalf. The young man Timothy would be a fellowship emissary of the incarcerated apostle. Prison bars could not restrict either Paul's or the church's joy.

Perhaps the discipline of emotional holiness must be found in both the now and the not-yet of fellowship with the saints. Even when Satan hindered Paul and his team's plans, the enemy had no authority over Paul's joy. He anticipated the final rejoicing at the Second Coming, but that final joy existed only as an extension of the glory and joy that Paul already experienced in the church. We can rest confident in a joy-filled eternity because we already practice this earnest of our inheritance now.

Healthy families enjoy each other's company and anticipate the next time they can be together. This measure of health only happens through shared experiences. Corporate worship services give one dimension of this fellowship, but delightful times around meals, common work projects, mutual support during trials, and missions endeavors must be a part of this joy-building enterprise. Just as surely as holy disciples would not think of dressing immodestly in public, they would not consider trying to serve as ambassadors by themselves. To do so would either succumb to a "hold the fort" mentality or arrogance of spiritual self-sufficiency.

Personal Reflection

1. *Fellowship is not the same thing as entertaining people. Reflect on a time where fellowship with others made a significant impact on your life. How did fellowship on that occasion differ from mere entertainment?*

2. *What are barriers to fellowship in your life? (For example, time, things in common, money, patterns of behavior, fear, etc.)*

3. *What fellowship skills do you need to develop? How could you develop those skills?*

Worship and Joy

God created human beings to be in constant fellowship with Him. In the Garden, people knew no obstacle to this fellowship. Talking with God was as natural as breathing air. Sin changed that. Sin brought separation and fear into what was once a delightful relationship. Joy changed to sorrow: sorrow in hiding from God, sorrow in childbirth, sorrow in work, and sorrow in relationships between people. Joy in relationship with the Creator also changed to fear of God's holiness.

The same process gets repeated throughout Scripture. For example, rather than seeking to draw near to God's presence on the mountain, the children of Israel sought a distant place and sent Moses to commune with God alone. The consequences included improper worship.

Avoiding God always leads to idolatry. Israel worshiped a golden calf. Even though they called the calf after the covenant name of God, they used wrongful worship to relieve the anxiety of their self-imposed separation. Israel fell just as Adam and Eve fell.

With the coming of Christ, we have the wonderful opportunity of restoring right worship. This worship should be found in absolutely every area of life. We worship in gathered times in the church sanctuary. We worship with a few friends around a meal where we bask in the wonder of being the people of God. We worship when we observe the beauty of the sunrise or a pod of dolphins leaping in the ocean. We worship as we go to bed at night and as we arise in the morning. We worship when a child is born and when a beloved saint passes on to glory. We worship when we give a beggar a drink of water and a ham-on-rye sandwich. Worshiping people live in constant awareness of God's nearness and goodness; they live to worship!

Israel and the early church used the Psalms to guide their worship. (See Ephesians 5:19.) While a full exploration of psalm genres exceeds the scope of this book, an examination of a few psalms demonstrates the relationship between right worship and right emotions. The very first psalm celebrates the blessings and delights of those who meditate on God's revealed law, day and night. Finding delight in God's Word provides both an anchor in the storm and the nutrients needed for a prosperous life. Those who worship God through meditating on the Word find joyful rest in the assurance that the Lord knows their way. While we do not worship God for these benefits, the discipline of worship produces great joy.

Authentic spiritual disciplines guide believers through times of suffering as well as times of productivity. Jesus quoted Psalm 22 in His own time of suffering. As a Jewish boy Jesus would have studied the Psalms to make worship a part of His emotional and spiritual DNA. Being immersed in the Psalms, He naturally cried out, "My God, my God, why hast thou forsaken me?" The point of death for all humanity's sin brought these words of anguish to His lips. The spiritual discipline of worship must include right ways to lament as well as right ways to rejoice. Dark days of the soul will come to all believers at one time or another. Survival depends on knowing how to lament well.

We should expect to worship in the context of observing nature. "The heavens declare the glory of God; and the firmament sheweth his handywork" (Psalm 19:1). Seeing the beasts of the forest and cattle on a farmer's hillside reminds us of the ultimate owner and calls us to offer thanksgiving and fulfillment of our commitments to God (Psalm 50:10–14). Observing fowl and fish calls for an exclamation of God's name (Psalm 8:8–9). God handed over the care of creation to men and women in the Garden of Eden. We must continue to worship Him as we see and care for His creative works in nature. In short, even the slightest observance of nature calls for at least a moment of worship. Some members of the body will answer the call to help us care for creation more faithfully and to witness to other leaders of ecological care who do not yet know the Creator. Some members of the body will answer the call to create works of art to arrest our attention in the mundane days and lift our gaze to see the heavenly artist's great masterpieces. Joy floods our souls as we worship well.

Ministry with a brother or sister produces worship and joy. Jesus sent out the seventy disciples in small ministry teams. Even though He sent them with few physical resources (not even change in the purse or an extra pair of shoes) they came back in a spirit of worship and great joy. Jesus joined in the worship as He recounted the spiritual truth that Satan continually fell as the small ministry teams sought those in need of peace and healing. The Teacher used the reflection moment to remind the seventy that they could always rejoice because their names were written in Heaven. We worship when ministry sees great results. We continue to worship when we see few immediate results. Such worship orients our emotions to find joy in service and in salvation. Such worship shelters our joy from counterclaims of society and our temptation to judge our value based on today's results.

Before we end this chapter, we must hear James's wise assessment of wrongful joy. (See James 4:7–17.) True joy comes from a right relationship with God and each other. The Cross inverted our efforts to achieve joy and pleasure. Jesus came as a humble servant and taught His students to do the same. James emphatically called his scattered church to walk in humility and to live as if they really believed life was short. True emotional holiness, as seen in joyful living, results from planning in line with the Lord's will. Even though James's comments directly related to the work of business people, all disciples must live within these principles.

Personal Reflection

Look around you right now and identify something that calls you to worship the Creator.

   a. *What would you include in a song, short story, poem, or work of art to describe this worship moment?*

   b. *How does this worship break affect your emotions?*

   c. *Prayerfully consider sharing your worship moment and creativity sketch with another believer. How might this process produce fellowship and joy as described in the last section?*

CONCLUSION

At one time people took IQ tests to gain entrance into some schools and workplaces. Those who scored below a certain mark may have been considered unsuitable for the program or job; they may have even needed financial and daily management assistance to help them function with some degree of independence. Other people were considered geniuses because of their ability to solve problems above the normal range. In the 1990s researchers began to explore intelligence in other areas such as interpersonal and kinesthetics. Recent research points to the value of emotional intelligence (EQ) in daily life as well as one's career.

Spiritual formation calls for examining our emotional holiness quotient (EHQ). While specific numbers cannot be assigned to our level of EHQ, individuals, families, and churches need to consider ways they can grow in emotional holiness. Assessing our ability to bless others, personal thanksgiving, living in hope, and joyful orientation to daily life situations calls us to put away childish behaviors and become mature disciples. EHQ questions directly address the degree of separation we have from the world's emotional dysfunction. If we find ourselves overwhelmed by fear, anxiety, anger, hopelessness, despair, or listlessness, then we need a season of spiritual formation directly related to emotional holiness.

As with all matters of holiness, we can be emotionally holy as we become more and more like Christ. We must do so as individuals as well as communities of believers. To ignore emotional holiness depletes our ability to give thanks to God and bless others. Being emotionally unholy squanders emotional and spiritual resources to just make it through the day; a low EHQ also squanders the church's resources by asking what the church can do for us rather than living missionally on behalf of the world. Finally, a church without maturing emotional holiness will not serve as a contrast people in the world. Emotional holiness witnesses to the blessed life of following Christ. Who would not want to join emotionally holy people who are following Christ?

PRAYER

I pray the Creator of Heaven and earth blesses you richly. I pray your eyes open even wider to the many gifts He has already given you. I pray your mind opens to the wonder of the completed Kingdom where all suffering ends, and that this awareness gives you the ability to despise the shame of this world just as Jesus did. I pray you receive the healing the Master chooses to give you now and the strength to live joyfully even in areas that He withholds the healing until the Last Day. I pray you live in a way that receives encouragement to mature emotionally even as you help others on this path. I pray we all live as a contrast people who worship the Master in every area of our lives.

In Jesus' name,
Amen

8 | *Repenting and Forgiving*

Spiritual formation calls us to listen to Jesus' examination of both the harms done toward others and responding to the breach caused by such actions. Spiritual formation enables us to listen to others and the Spirit in the most challenging of times. Listening enables us to follow Jesus and receive His grace rather than reacting to harmful acts of others or responding out of our pain. Being like Christ brings healing and restoration to all who choose to follow Him.

In Matthew 5 Jesus explained the ways in which He came to fulfill the Law. In doing so, the Teacher examined both the Ten Commandments and ways human tradition added to the Law. Jesus traced most of the cases back to the heart and called for His disciples to address the underlying cause rather than avoiding the behavior that caused pain. Rather than ratifying the Law's prohibition of murder, Jesus stated labeling someone a fool placed the perpetrator of slander in danger of hell fire (Matthew 5:22). While calling someone *raca* or "fool" seems like a mild statement of anger many of us have used when cut off in traffic or upset by carelessness of a brother or sister, Jesus saw calling someone worthless or empty as an attack on the personhood of the victim. At the root of the harm is the attack on the image of God that resides in every person and people group.

Jesus provided the means for addressing slander of the image of God in the next few verses. He urgs us to be reconciled with those we have harmed as we prepare to offer our gifts at the altar (Matthew 5:23–24). In other words, the call to worship includes the call to examine our relationships with others. We cannot love the God we have not seen while hating the brother we have seen (I John 4:20). If we hate a brother, or even call someone a fool, then Christ is not ready to receive our offering. Consider for a moment what would happen if we changed our prayers for offerings next Sunday. What would be the response if we prayed, "Father, show us the way our offering and worship is rejected if we do not seek healing of our relationships. Give us the courage to pause in worship to repent to those we have harmed. Give us the strength to forgive others as You have forgiven us." I believe the first couple offerings would be smaller than when we pray the typical, "Bless those who have to give and those who do not have to give."

Everyone reading this book has had the opportunity to verify Jesus' words in Matthew 18:7: "Woe unto the world because of offenses! For it must needs be that offenses come; but woe to that man by whom the offense cometh!" I pray none have taken the next step of hyperbole mentioned by Jesus—to cut off a limb to prevent further offense. Fortunately, the gospel's good news lets us know someone else already paid a heavy price to transform our behavior.

Spiritual formation calls disciples to surrender to Jesus' model of reconciliation rather than that of the world. By doing so we become more like Him. The Teacher gave concise instructions for the process of restoring relationships in Luke 17:3–5. "Take heed to yourselves: if thy brother trespass against thee, rebuke him, and if he repent, forgive him. And if he trespass against thee seven times in a day, and seven times in a day turn again to thee saying, I repent; thou shalt forgive him."

Our examination of the disciplines of repentance and forgiveness will follow the conditional clauses carefully set up by Jesus.

✓ If a person trespasses against you,
    then rebuke them.

✓ If they repent,
    then forgive them.

Jesus reveals the process He follows in restoring humanity to a right relationship with Him. Following Jesus' example reminds us of the goal of all spiritual formation—to become more like our Teacher. In challenging times, we will be tempted to rely on our ability to forgive and forget because the pain can be so numbing. Forgiveness places us firmly in a new wave of grace. Jesus will be with us as we learn to walk like Him.

OFFENSES WILL COME

Since Charles Darwin introduced concepts of evolution to explain his perception of life sciences in his influential *On the Origin of Species by Means of Natural Selection, or The Preservation of Favoured Races in the Struggle for Life* in 1859, people have wondered what separates human beings from other life forms. The debate has led so far as the proposal of speciesism, human discrimination against other life forms on the basis of absence or presence of various characteristics. I am assuming a majority of the readers of this book would prefer to have a pet dog or cat than a pet brown recluse spider. People have valued certain aspects of dogs over arachnids and thus give them more privilege or respect. One can be arrested for cruelty to dogs, but homeowners are well within their rights to get rid of dangerous spiders.

While exploring the differences between humans and nonhuman creatures goes way beyond the scope of this book, perhaps considering the human condition of suffering could be a part of the distinction. Biblically we see humanity placed in the Garden to care for all creatures. With the human decision to trespass against God's one limit on their behavior—do not eat of that one tree—all of creation suffered and continues to suffer from secondhand effects of sin. Human beings seem to excel in bringing harm to each other and to the creation God designed them to lovingly superintend. Some offenses are intentional, and others may come from mere neglect.

Living out Kingdom possibilities provides the opportunity to give and receive forgiveness as a consequence of our newfound relationship with our Creator. In this process we become more like Christ. Human efforts to solve offenses will always result in limited, though worthy, outcomes. Society tries to punish perpetrators with shame, fines, imprisonment, loss of civil rights, exile, or even death, yet crime continues. Psychologists and other helping professions can provide strategies for getting out of harm's way as well as minimizing some of the effects of harm as diverse as bullying, domestic violence, racial bias, post-traumatic stress disorder, and classism, but the problems seem to outstrip the tools and time of dedicated individuals and professions. As with other broken aspects of the human condition, the only lasting solution is to return to the Creator's plan. We hear His voice, follow His example, and receive grace as we become more like Him.

Repentance and forgiveness begin with serving the Lord. Our ability to experience healing relationships serves as a major component of our witness to the world. Jesus said His disciples would be identified by their love for one another (John 13:35). Paul echoed this principle as well when he admonished the church to settle their disputes among themselves rather than going to the civil court system. (See I Corinthians 6.) While the principles in Jesus' forgiveness model can be applied to non–Christ-centered relationships, the process may not always be effective. We can forgive one another because we have received forgiveness from above. He has graced us to become more like Him.

The first step of this spiritual discipline involves giving thanks again for the many ways God has forgiven us. While grace is always available, in thanksgiving disciples make themselves more aware of the waves of grace.

The second step consists of identifying areas where we have harmed others. As you identify those areas prepare yourself to go to the offended party as an act of humble worship. Humility places us in a right relationship with others and with God. You will be able to confess your wrong, seek reconciliation, and pursue more holy responses in the future because you prefer God's good purposes rather than defending your own pride.

The third step requires us to address areas where we have suffered at the hands of brothers and sisters. We have the capacity to do so because Jesus has showed us the way. He too received wounds at the hands of His friends: wounds when family thought He suffered from delusions, wounds when Jerusalem rejected His offering of care, wounds from active betrayal by Judas, wounds from the tribunal and power-broker sympathizers, wounds from those "just doing their job" in driving the nails, and wounds of abandonment by others. His wounds defy cataloging.

The fourth step requires us to lay down our prerogatives in this process and accept Jesus' purposes for repentance and forgiveness. Jesus' work will point out abuse and harm because He seeks to bring reconciliation to all broken parts of the human condition. Jesus wants His body to be put back together again. This work of reconciliation will result in personal hope and happiness, but those personal outcomes cannot be the goal of the process. Pursuing the Christlike objectives of spiritual formation places faith in God's healing, hope, and honor rather than experiencing more pain, despair, and shame that comes when we try to fix things on our own.

Prayer

I pray the Lord gives you the strength to celebrate the wonder of divine forgiveness you have received. I pray the Spirit gives you the courage to admit places where you have left a brother or sister in pain and just walked away. I pray the seed of faith begins to take root in your life to aid you in identifying the hurt and shame you have suffered at the hands of others. I pray you feel the Teacher's loving embrace in all these things as you pursue your Christlike identity. I pray you trust His grace will bring the healing you may need.

In Jesus' name,
Amen

Personal Reflection

*Review the primary points from the first
section of chapter 8. Honestly examine your
relationship with others. Make notes for your
next prayer time. If you experience any pain, despair,
or shame, confess those emotions to the One who can
handle them. Pray for the strength to follow Jesus' words
and examples as you seek to be more like Him. Finally
give thanks for the grace you feel as you walk with Him.*

LOVING REBUKE

I do not know of anyone who likes to be rebuked. Many of us do not like to confront others any more than we like to be personally confronted. We must remember that the goals of spiritual formation always come from above. If confrontation is about proving we are more right, better people, or more spiritual than the person we must confront, then we start with the wrong foundation and will cause more harm than good.

Perhaps *carefrontation* would be a better way to understand this process. Just as God so loves us that He convicts us through the Spirit, Word, and community of believers, He is sending us to lovingly *carefront* those who have harmed us. As Christ graciously cares for us, He sends us to care for one another.

One way to consider a biblical perspective on godly rebuke starts with the role of prophets in the Old Testament. Prophets spoke to the people or to individuals on God's behalf. Often the prophets served a role to call kings and other leaders back to a more faithful relationship to

God. For example, II Samuel 12 relates Nathan's care for David after he committed adultery with Bathsheba and murdered her husband, Uriah the Hittite. Nathan fearlessly spoke up on behalf of the powerless and the dead who were not able to speak on their own behalf. Scripture frequently calls God's people to righteous living where the poor, marginalized, strangers, widows, and fatherless cannot speak for themselves. Nathan's godly rebuke, given at the risk of his own life, resulted in King David's repentance and restoration to right standing before God.

While the church still needs to speak and do justice on behalf of those who cannot speak for themselves, our discussion of spiritual formation through repentance and forgiveness will consider the personal relationships between men and women of faith. To love a brother or sister includes the willingness to lovingly rebuke them when they have harmed you.

People who pray, "Thy kingdom come, Thy will be done," have chosen to follow the Prince of Peace's desire for love in His kingdom. Kingdom spiritual formation calls us to live out the King's purposes now in accordance with what He has already identified as His good pleasure for eternity. Suffering and tears have no place in Heaven. Suffering and strife must begin to give way now. Following Christ and seeking to be like Him provides the grace and strength needed to pursue reconciliation where His children have experienced deep, painful divisions. The Book of James addresses divisions in the body of Christ as part of lack of faith. Walking in faith results in healing in the body—healing that respects people of all classes and abilities. Saints may suffer because of their missionary lives in the world, but they should not suffer in the body. James includes the call to confess and pray for one another as a means of healing just as he speaks of elders praying with oil. (See James 5:13–16.) The apostle ends his epistle with a call to carefront errors and sin in the body; such care-frontations have the capacity to "hide a multitude of sins" (James 5:20).

Loving rebuke always springs from care for the body. Christ calls us to act lovingly toward those who abuse us. When harm comes between brothers and sisters in Christ, then we must love them enough to rebuke them. Loving rebuke assists one's own spiritual formation, the spiritual formation of the abuser, and the spiritual climate of the whole church. The goal is to witness the eternal principles of faith, hope, and love flourish in a dark and evil world. Grace provides the power and way through this difficult time.

As we come to the end of this section, let's consider a real-life case study that will help us concretely apply Jesus' teaching in an effort to become more like Him. A young adult expressed her hurt to a spiritual leader in her life. Perhaps the hurt included layers of anger as well. She shared her pain at the hand of a fellow saint who consistently exhibited racist tendencies toward her. She knew she should not feel shame for being black; she also knew unresolved anger would not help her to grow as one of God's beloved daughters. Over the course of several discussions, the leader helped her explore the nature of the abuse and identify steps she could take to be like Christ. She had to lovingly rebuke the fellow saint for the racist remarks even when he did not fully grasp the evil behind his words. She had to trust the

Spirit's leading to bring a positive resolution to the issue. Grace paved the way.

Personal Reflection

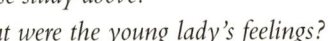

Consider the following questions as you think about the case study above:

a. *What were the young lady's feelings?*

b. *Why did the hurtful remarks attack the Creator?*

c. *How did the leader help her understand her emotions?*

d. *What was the end goal that led their discussion and action steps?*

e. *How do you think God's grace assisted the leader? The young lady?*

CONTRITE REPENTANCE

Repentance serves as a key foundational principle for all of God's people. We repented as part of our new birth experience. Both John the Baptist and Jesus included repentance as key elements of their messages. For John, repentance included measurable components such as fruit production (Luke 3:8). For Jesus, repentance directly connected to the inbreaking of the Kingdom and believing the gospel (Mark 1:15). Peter made sure his audience realized that repentance included turning toward God and resulted in conversion with sins being "wiped out" (Acts 3:19). Unchanged behavior would not be real repentance.

Repentance calls us to surrender to God's purposes and will. We delight in knowing His ways are superior to ours and can quickly repent when we recognize we have stepped out of His ways. Repentance calls us to see God's desire for us through the words and works of others in addition to those written in Scripture. When lovingly rebuked by a brother or sister, our natural inclination might be defensiveness or cold silence. Our new creaturely inclination must be listening for God's voice through the words of someone who loves us enough to point out our offense.

In the racism case mentioned above, the rebuked saint had to hear the words of the sister who was speaking words of righteousness and love. He could not defend his comments as something that just came from his cultural background. He had to realize his comments brought painful division whether he meant it for ill or not. The carefronting sister had to walk with him through the uncovering phase of the process. The perpetrator had to understand the layers of hurt experienced by the victim and own up to his own role in the process.

A desire to be like Christ set the trajectory for both the offender and the victim. The victim sought restoration for the broken relationship. The offender confessed the harm brought to the body by his individual action. He received the words of Christ through the sister. Spiritual formation brought both closer to Christ.

In the contrition phase of repentance, the offender must confess and ask for forgiveness. This spiritual formation process may take time and ongoing sessions of uncovering the sources of the hurting behavior. The difficult process is possible because we have all repented to

God and because we commit to living together as God's people. As with loving rebuke, confession and repentance is not about gaining the spiritual higher ground, holding the other person in a debt, or gaining closure as quickly as possible. Instead, repentance provides a step toward healing for both the offender and the victim as the Lord brings reconciliation in His body. A reconciled body can witness love and peace in a chaotic world.

Personal Reflection

Reflect on the case study. How did the victim and offender become more like Christ in the repentance phase?

FORGIVING LIKE CHRIST

For forgiveness to fulfill its spiritual formation function, we must follow God's example. We forgive each other as God has forgiven us. God's forgiveness includes reconciliation between the sinner and a holy God. Paul's relationship with the Corinthian church suffered a number of strains over a period of years. In II Corinthians 2 we can still hear the apostle's plea for forgiveness in the body. Without forgiveness, Paul said two direct outcomes could happen: (1) the perpetrator would be "swallowed up with overmuch sorrow" (II Corinthians 2:7), and (2) "Satan should get an advantage of us" (II Corinthians 2:11). We can also deduce from his words that withholding forgiveness would leave one's love and obedience in question (verses 8–9). God had forgiven Paul of much, thus he ably forgave "in the person of Christ" (verse 10).

Christ's incarnation becomes a present reality in forgiveness. In His teaching, Jesus confirmed the relationship between us forgiving one another and our ongoing forgiven status with the Father. (See, for example, Mark 11:25–26.) Forgiveness, in the way Jesus used the term, always includes restoration of relationship. When the Father forgives us, we wonderfully experience restored relationship with Him. In fact, living out this forgiven state continues to deepen that relationship with God and with others. The Spirit helps us forgive just as we are forgiven.

Perhaps this brings us to the hard part of the spiritual formation of forgiveness: we cannot experience reconciliatory forgiveness with those who do not seek restored relationship. Reconciliatory forgiveness follows the example we experience when God forgives us. As we have seen above, Luke 17:3 sets repentance as a precondition of forgiveness. In our case study we can imagine an alternate ending where the brother did not repent. Even though the sister would have prayed and lovingly called the brother to repent of ungodly racism, he could have refused the invitation to become more like Christ. This sad ending would not have resulted in reconciliatory forgiveness.

God forgives us when we repent. As nice as it sounds to simply forgive others for their wrong behavior, such forgiveness, that is forgiveness not linked to repentance, hinders the perpetrator from finding spiritual restoration he or she desperately needs. In Mark 11:22–26 Jesus gave powerful instruction on faith-filled prayers. Mountains could be moved by those who believe. Jesus gave two conditions that hinder such prayer. Doubt robs the believer of much power. Refusal to forgive goes even further: power is lost along with the promise of the Father's forgiveness. Jesus once again drew the direct relationship between God's forgiveness and our own. Forgiveness restores relationships with God, and it will do the same in the body of Christ. Restored relationship guarantees flow out of our own forgiveness. Fortunately, Jesus gave the step-by-step instructions in Luke 17.

Before moving to the next element of this spiritual formation task, we need to examine the nature of forgiveness a little more deeply. While God can forgive us in an instant and can bring about instant restoration of relationship, we usually cannot do an instant work of forgiveness. Just as a repentant person honestly seeks to turn around in the relationship and live in accordance with the loving relationship, a forgiving person must realize the extended nature of the forgiveness process. Many people confess forgiveness, but they experience confusion at the ongoing separation they feel. The initial forgiveness statement serves as a pledge, commitment, and faith that forgiveness will be completed. We do so because Christ is present with us; the Spirit helps us live into what we have spoken.

The work phase of repentance and forgiveness makes restoration possible. The perpetrator gains insight into his or her behavior. The roots of the evil action or mean-spirited word get exposed and destroyed. The victim gains strength from his or her own forgiveness from God and moves toward resolution. The shame or evil loses its power to control emotions and actions. Both parties find meaning and purpose in the forgiveness process.

Personal Reflection

1. *What barriers do you face in spiritual formation when you are the victim?*

2. *What barriers do you face in spiritual formation when you are the perpetrator?*

3. *What steps can you take to become more like Christ?*

4. *Consider cultural values that stand against the process of becoming more like Christ. How does the gospel call for transformation in your value allegiance?*

CHURCH DISCIPLINE

Jesus never sends His people to do His work without going with them. Incarnational spiritual formation, formation to live out our missional purposes here rather than just to be ready for Heaven, provides an opportunity to see the Spirit at work in everyday life. Sometimes a member of the body does not respond to the loving rebuke of the one she has harmed. In fact, the perpetrator sometimes makes the victim feel even more shame by refusing to acknowledge the sin and placing the blame on the victim for not "just letting it go." In those moments Christ will certainly be present.

A church body intent on incarnational spiritual formation will know Christ shows up in difficult times. Since we know humans will hurt one another from time to time, we should follow the biblical plan to turn Satan's trap into a spiritual formation opportunity. Perhaps we hear

Matthew 18:20 quoted at the beginning of worship services or prayer meetings with low attendance. Certainly, Jesus is there, "For where two or three are gathered together in my name, there am I in the midst of them" rings true in times of corporate worship regardless of the number in attendance. The context of Jesus' promise, however, deals with the difficulties of church discipline and forgiving one another. Jesus committed to be present in the midst of repentance and forgiveness in a special way because He came to bring reconciliation. Jesus wants us to be more like Him.

A church culture of loving rebuke, contrite repentance, and Christlike forgiveness sets the conditions for this spiritual formation process. While all of Matthew 18 helps us understand the process, verse 15 and subsequent verses set out the steps to pursue. The first step includes the individual intervention outlined in this chapter. If the perpetrator will not respond to the victim's efforts, then a witness or two should be invited into the process. If the small committee cannot help the perpetrator see the error of his or her ways and celebrate the gift of repentance, then the larger church body will be involved in the process. Perhaps the church can be represented by the church's board of deacons or a special spiritual care team. At every step of the way, Jesus will be present to help bring about restoration and healing. If the perpetrator refuses to repent and grow spiritually, then the church leaders may need to separate the person from the body. This is the context for "binding and loosing" (Matthew 18:18–19). The objective must always revolve around the incarnational work of reconciliation. The ultimate aim of removing a person from the body is for the unrepentant person to seek restoration at some point and to repent.

Churches that teach and practice repentance and forgiveness help saints in their daily lives. Learning submission in the body helps in family life and other contexts of living as we see in Paul's household codes. Paul encouraged appropriate behavior in the context of following God, as did Jesus. Jesus gave priority to obeying the Father's words rather than familial relationships even though this violated cultural norms. Church life should help us bear one another's burdens even while we bear our own burdens. In that context, the spiritually mature saints will be able to more effectively restore those "overtaken in a fault" (Galatians 6:1–5).

JESUS THE HEALER

Another challenge with forgiveness rests in cases where the perpetrator has died. Some Christians suggest going to the graveyard and forgiving the abuse of a parent, friend, or spiritual leader who lies beneath the ground. The suggestion comes from the need to overcome the hurt of past abuse and shame, from an effort to end the abuse, and to bring about healing or psychic closure. While the motives and end goals are positive, true reconciliation is no longer possible. God's desire for restoration of all things cannot be fulfilled in that specific case due to the death of one of the estranged parties. This statement could lead to hopelessness if we did not know the Healer.

Sadly, some people will refuse to participate in the incarnational work of grace present in repentance and forgiveness. When the perpetrator refuses to repent, the victim may continue to suffer from shame and pain. In this case, the victim needs to remember she has a Healer that has been touched by her infirmities. The following steps can be a useful guide in the healing process. These same steps will help those who cannot carefront a person who has already passed away.

As with all spiritual formation, the goal of healing is to be more like Christ rather than healing of the pain. While the relationship will not be restored at this time as God intended with the Luke 17 process, the victim will experience healing and will be effectively released from spiritual and emotional barriers to ministry effectiveness. Like Christ, we can stay on the reconciliation mission even when we experience rejection.

First the victim needs to search his own heart one more time. Examining the heart rejects the cultural suggestion to "follow your heart." Spiritual formation rejects this axiom because we know the heart cannot be trusted to speak the truth (Jeremiah 17:9). In prayer, meditation on the Word, and in confession with a trusted spiritually mature person, the victim makes sure he is not at fault in the matter. If the Spirit reveals a previously unseen root of the problem in the victim's life, then that person will need to go and repent to whomever he has wronged. If the victim still finds no fault in his own life, then that person is ready to move to the second step.

Next the victim commits to letting God be the judge and defender of justice. Followers of Jesus surrender the role of judge to the One who has a better perspective and who will hold all unrighteousness accountable in the judgment. The victim refuses to let personal emotions or Satan propel him to seek revenge.

The victim will go one step further in surrendering the person to the hands of the Judge—the spiritually mature victim will begin to intercede on behalf of the one who has sinned against him, as did Jesus and Stephen.

Finally, the victim can petition the gracious God for healing. In this step God's lavish love can be experienced afresh after having let go of the victim status in the previous step. Sensitivities to offending behaviors may continue, but those sensitivities will be a resource in caring for others who suffer, rather than in seeking personal vengeance. The outcome of healing will be like forgiveness in some ways and different in others. No longer will the past control present or future emotions and spirit. The victim can think of the perpetrator without shame or pain. Healing will probably not include reconciliation, however, unless the perpetrator decides at some point to repent.

Personal Reflection

Identify sources of hurt you have suffered when someone has refused to engage in the reconciliation process or has passed away. Share your source of pain with a spiritually mature person. Ask that person to walk with you through the healing steps identified above. Receive healing from the One who fully understands your pain.

CONCLUSION

Perhaps the spiritual formation of repentance and forgiveness takes one closer to the heart of God than any of the other spiritual formation processes in this book. Maybe this is why forgiveness is so challenging. This chapter undoubtedly stirs emotions, raises questions, and may even leave a reader feeling emotionally exhausted. These responses flow from being close to God's heart, the place of reconciliation. When Jesus explained this process to His disciples in Luke 17:3–5, the spiritual and emotional response mirrors our own. "Lord, Increase our faith!"

Jesus sent His disciples to heal the sick and to cast out devils. We frequently judge how much faith we have in our ability to do those two elements of spiritual warfare. We rightly value people of faith who have healing ministries and capably push back the enemy through their prayer lives. What would happen if we prayed for faith in the same place where the disciples did? Surely the Lord would be gathered together with us. Surely we would be able to loose and bind in the spirit world. Surely we would have fewer divisions in the churches, families, and even across Apostolic denominations. Surely we could confidently experience Jesus' healing touch when we suffer as He did and do not hear folks repent. Surely we can live overcoming lives freed from oppression, victimization, and a quest to prove ourselves valuable to other people.

PRAYER

I pray the Lord graces you richly with incarnational faith, faith lived out in relationships. I pray you feel the nearness of God's heartbeat as you do the work of reconciliation in repentance and in forgiveness. I pray you resist the easier paths suggested by civil religion. I pray the Father's kingdom come and will be done as you experience reconciliation in the real world.

In Jesus' name,

Amen

9 | *Simplicity and Stewardship*

The Teacher formed His disciples through a variety of well-chosen methods—timeless methods equally valid today. One day He chose a street-mugging story to drive home the priority of loving God and loving neighbors. A story about street violence did not faze His audience. No, the Teacher shocked everyone by valuing the efforts of a Samaritan.

Samaritans had similar roots to the Jewish inhabitants of Jerusalem, but their differences in theology and practices set them apart, and many Jews viewed them with disdain. Jesus did not laud the Samaritan's faith, instead He used the example of a "good" Samaritan to underscore His main point—those who love God must be a neighbor to all who are near and in need. Neighborly love has more to do with meeting needs and less to do with the relationship. Jesus echoed this principle in another place when He told the disciples to love everyone, even their enemies. (See Matthew 5:43–45.)

We must care for others because of their need rather than our common identity. Being neighborly proves inconvenient for busy people. The priest and Levite did not have time to care for the mugged man even though they knew benevolence served as a key component of their faith. They were more worried about the danger of muggers lingering nearby or the possibility of becoming unclean by coming into contact with blood or a dead person than they were concerned about the welfare of the injured man. They exercised stewardship of their position rather than stewardship of their resources. The Good Samaritan, on the other hand, was willing to share generously with the person in need: time to provide care, finances to provide both emergency and follow-up care without asking the cost, and even follow-up care on the return trip.

Spiritual formation invites disciples to discover the treasures in their hands, evaluate the needs around them, and serve others in an effort to be more like their Teacher. Following Jesus will always require a lifestyle makeover. When Zacchaeus opened his dining parlor to Jesus, everything changed. When salvation crossed his threshold, he changed his priorities. Rather than protecting his image or position, he opened his life. Rather than hoarding his wealth or expanding his tax-collecting franchise, the new disciple gave away a large portion of his wealth and began a comprehensive audit of his business practices. Similarly, our spiritual formation revolutionizes our priorities as we become stewards of God's gifts in our lives.

Personal Reflection

The Parable of the Good Samaritan calls us to examine our stewardship focus in light of loving Jesus.

   a. *How was the priest faithful to his priestly office in avoiding the unclean situation?*

b. *How might his Temple ministry have suffered had he loved the injured man in accordance with Jesus' teaching?*

c. *How might the priest's day and week have changed had he expended resources on behalf of the neighbor?*

d. *How does Jesus' teaching call us to privilege stewardship of resources over stewardship of position or office? How does the Spirit call you to respond to this principle?*

THE FAITHFULNESS RULE

I have to resist pulling off the highway to read every historical marker. In some parts of the US, one might think George Washington stayed overnight in every old house. Other historical signs commemorate battles between the Union and Confederate armies during the US Civil War. I have read a number of signs that tell of the First Nations or Native American tribes that historically lived in that area. Perhaps the most telling sign was one that said, "Absolutely Nothing Ever Happened Here."

Some people have a Napoleon complex in which they feel the need to rule the world, while others doubt the world would ever notice if they ceased to exist. People, like geographical locations, have different measures of self-worth. Those who choose to answer Jesus' invitation to follow Him will have to reassess their measuring tools. Just as different instruments must be used to measure the thickness of a sheet of paper and the distance from the sun to the earth, disciples must make sure they use the appropriate instrument to measure their value.

The first step in the instrument selection process identifies who has the right to determine the value. Just as miners take ore samples to an assayer to determine the potential value of a mine, disciples must surrender themselves to the assayer of life. Paul tried to help the Corinthian saints reframe their understanding of Kingdom measurement principles. Instead of seeking God's approval, the Corinthian church used assessment rubrics such as powerful rhetoric, worldly wisdom, and patronage systems. Paul showed them a better way: God would dwell in them, and they would serve as living temples of God. He alone would determine their worth.

The second step in instrument selection depends on grasping the criteria the evaluator wants to use. A judge for the county fair uses a different system of evaluating 4-H club member cows than the system a chef at an exclusive restaurant would use. They both judge cows. They use different criteria. Over the course of my thirty-five years as an educator at nearly all grade levels, I have had occasions to use several different evaluation philosophies. While grading papers, whether for my fifth-grade English class or a second-year graduate course, I often used a holistic grading schedule. As the evaluator, I had expectations for an excellent paper, a good paper, an acceptable paper, and a paper that could not receive a grade at all. The grade would be for the whole paper, rather than separate points for different parts of the assignment. At other times I would design a rubric where every aspect of the assignment would be graded with clear expectations for a number of points for each item. I gave students the rubric with the assignment; they began the assignment knowing exactly how I would evaluate them. In both cases, I tried to evaluate all students in the same course with a consistent standard.

God alone has the right to set the standard and evaluate His servants. Rather than using the Old Testament law and its 613 specific rules, the New Testament follows a more holistic evaluation of our use of the resources the Master places at our disposal. Before Paul could address spiritual gifts in I Corinthians 12–14, he had to convince his readers to recognize one standard exists for all disciples.

Faithfulness.

That is it; faithfulness alone.

Galatians provides a case study for those who think faithfulness fails to reflect a good enough standard. In an effort to "improve" on the Master's plan, they tried to layer measurable works on top of faith's response to grace. Paul said they had been bewitched or drugged. He thought he may have to give birth to them a second time.

Faithfulness alone makes some people nervous. I am one of those people. Maybe I stayed in school until age forty-two because the expectations and rewards were clearly defined. Following the Teacher, however, calls me to trust Him more than I trust anyone or anything else in this world. I must trust that He knows what He is doing when He calls us together to be His disciples. I must trust that He works through us to continue His reconciliation process. He places disciples in the body according to His divine plan. He wisely gifts each part of the body with different resources as it labors as one unit. We all get a measure of faith, but we do not all get the same gracious gifting.

Adopting a clear-cut, multiple-category evaluation tool to cover all disciples would not work. Imagine if people judged all athletes by the same standard. How could we evaluate long-distance runners and sumo wrestlers on the same scale? We would have to reduce all athletes to one dimension rather than many different forms of athleticism. The Master values all His disciples and gifts them differently.

Paul introduced faithfulness as the only standard the Master uses to evaluate His stewards. Everything else abuses some of His students and falsely promotes others. Other standards question His ability to know the needs of the world and His body. "It is required in stewards, that a man be found faithful" (I Corinthians 4:2). Stewards own nothing; rather, they take responsibility of the resources trusted to their care. Stewards cannot judge themselves. Stewards can assist one another in being faithful, but they cannot judge each other. Faithfulness to the Master represents the highest standard. To whom much is given, much is required.

The process of spiritual formation may uncover inappropriate standards we have used to measure our stewardship. Competition, personal recognition, earning right standing before God, and past performance are all inappropriate standards. We must lay aside these standards and pursue simply being faithful.

Stewardship includes a call to worship. When we worship the Lord, then we can freely acknowledge our place as servants. Worship acknowledges God's ability to see, plan, and carry out His will according to His good pleasure. It reminds us of the beauty of faithfulness and enables us to walk with other faithful stewards.

Stewardship calls us to value all our resources as property of the Master. To reject our gifts would be to distrust the Master who equips His servants according to His good pleasure. This chapter provides an opportunity to take inventory of our resources and focus those resources on the Master's purposes.

Stewardship calls us to faithfulness. But faithfulness doesn't happen overnight. Becoming a faithful steward takes effort, time, a community of saints, and the work of the Spirit.

Personal Reflection

1. *What are the standards of success in your workplace, school, or home?*

2. *How does biblical stewardship differ from those models?*

3. *What are some potential consequences of the differences between your culture's standards and Kingdom standards?*

SIMPLICITY

As a child I enjoyed visiting Howes Caverns in New York. What wonderful beauty came from thousands of years of dripping water! I could not believe the colorful stalactites and stalagmites resulted from microscopic collections of limestone. Some scientists estimate water would need to drip for one thousand years to form ten centimeters of stalactite. Perhaps God created an "old earth" with wonderful caverns that continue to form until this day.

Unfortunately, Americans find buildup of "stuff" in their lives accumulates at a much faster rate. Even though many houses and apartments in the US and Canada are large compared to most dwellings around the world, some people still need additional storage space to handle the spillover of all their good stuff. Industry estimates an annual self-storage revenue of $22 billion derived from fifty-eight thousand facilities that average 566 units each. About 9 percent of US households keep these facilities 87 percent occupied each year. That does not count basements, attics, garages, outbuildings, and other places we pack with our stuff.

Spiritual formation calls for valuing simplicity enough to practice the discipline. Simplicity and decluttering may be a cultural phenomenon at this point in our history, but disciples' motivations differ from their neighbors. Jesus asked Peter if he loved stuff more than he loved his Teacher. Jesus had to ask three times to finally get the point through to one of His prize students. Unless Peter loved Jesus more than stuff, he would not be able to fulfill his place in the body of disciples. Peter had to surrender his natural inclination to want stuff if he truly wanted to love the Teacher; otherwise he would be disqualified from feeding sheep. (See John 21.)

In the Sermon on the Mount, Jesus gave the principles and motivations for practicing the stewardship discipline of simplicity. Treasures in this life lose their value due to moths and rust; their owners must invest a significant amount of money on security systems to keep the thieves away. Placing value on worldly treasures marks a difference between disciples and everybody else. Disciples place their treasures in Heaven. By selecting a heavenly storage facility, disciples place their hearts in a singular place—a place filled with divine light. Refusing to practice earthly treasure displacement results in a power outage, a place of total darkness. In fact, failure to destroy the gods of stuff leaves a person trying to serve two masters. Such efforts lead to miserable failure.

Nonbelievers concern themselves with stuff. Jesus continued His stewardship teaching by calling His students to turn from cluttered quests for food, drink, and clothing. Rather than being preoccupied with even these bare necessities of life, following the Teacher releases every student to the far greater priority of seeking "first the kingdom of God, and his righteousness" (Matthew 6:33). He gave the reason for this acquisition makeover: "For your heavenly Father knoweth that ye have need of these things" (Matthew 6:32).

In Scripture God consistently called faithful people to flourish within their limits rather than seeking to acquire more things. Such biblical principles seem heretical to the Western mind. American culture thrives on creating dissatisfaction in its citizenry. The economy would be shaken if people started being satisfied with what they have and where they live.

The psalmist worshiped the Lord by confessing his satisfaction with his inheritance and the boundaries in his life. (See Psalm 16:5–9.) The psalmist modeled a wonderful path to experience what Paul would express as "godliness with contentment is great gain" (I Timothy 6:6). Perhaps Paul's evaluation of life sounds even more overwhelming when one reads the apostle's context. Paul called servants to honor their masters so "that the name of God and his doctrine be not blasphemed" (6:1). In fact, when disciples encounter people teaching acquisition as an artifact of godliness, they should withdraw from those folks (6:5).

Psalm 16 provides important components of separating ourselves from a world focused on obtaining more stuff.

- Recognizing the beauty of the current location

- Blessing the Lord in that location

- Pursuing the Lord's counsel rather than the spirits of this world

- Having a heart that turns one in the right direction rather than self-justification

- Following closely behind the Lord

- Realizing the power that comes from treasuring the Lord as the source of strength in the current circumstances

In what condition would you find yourself if you followed Paul and the psalmist's advice? Certainly the outcomes in Psalm 16:9 demonstrate the consequences of a life well-lived: "Therefore my heart is glad, and my glory [tongue] rejoiceth: my flesh also shall rest in hope."

The Lord has indeed given us a wonderful inheritance as sons and daughters. The prophet Isaiah provided powerful reminders of the Lord's lavish love toward His people: "No weapon that is formed against thee shall prosper; and every tongue that shall rise against thee in judgment thou shalt condemn. This is the heritage of the servants of the LORD, and their righteousness is of me, saith the LORD" (Isaiah 54:17).

The spiritual discipline of simplicity brings Jesus' students closer to their Teacher. He began in a borrowed manger, lived with no place to lay His head, and was buried in someone else's tomb. He also fulfilled all the Father sent Him to do. What would happen if disciples supported each other in simplifying their lives around daily pursuing God's purposes?

Personal Reflection

The simple life happens by taking small steps.
   a. *Identify one area of your life that you want to declutter in Jesus' name.*

   b. *Select small, practical steps you can take on a daily or weekly basis to accomplish this goal.*

   c. *Share your plan with another decluttering disciple. Meet with that disciple after a few weeks to examine your progress.*

   d. *What challenges did you encounter? What joys did you experience? Where has the Spirit led you to declutter next?*

   e. *Be sure to celebrate even the small opportunities to serve neighbors in need with your newfound resources.*

TALENTS

When God got to one of His final acts of creation, He chose to make men and women in His own image. While theologians and biblical scholars have debated the exact characteristics God molded into human beings, we can stand in awe of the opportunity to carry parts of that image. We image God more completely when we work together than we do on our own. By pooling our callings, giftings, talents, and living as one body, we "may grow up into him in all things, which is the head, even Christ: from whom the whole body fitly joined together and compacted by that which every joint supplieth, according to the effectual working in the measure of every part, maketh increase of the body unto the edifying of itself in love" (Ephesians 4:15–16).

While we all carry the image of God in some way, we fail to live out our potential unless we steward those resources together. Conversely, when every disciple intentionally cares for personal talents and giftings, then the body lives up to its Head's purposes. Periodically, every disciple will need to evaluate his or her efficacy in developing those talents and using them for God's purposes. Ultimately our good gifts all come from above and belong to the One who distributes those gifts according to His good pleasure. We should not dread the accounting day when He judges everyone's works. (See I Corinthians 3:10–16.)

God has blessed us with brothers and sisters we can consult in this evaluation process. For example, Paul blessed Timothy by sharing his perceptions of the younger man's stewardship effectiveness. Paul knew Timothy's spiritual heritage and his gifts. He cared enough about Timothy's stewardship to call him back to the moment when Timothy received the laying on of hands. Paul gave simple admonishment: "Wherefore I put thee in remembrance that thou stir up the gift of God, which is in thee by the putting on of my hands" (II Timothy 1:6).

Whether or not we had godly mothers and grandmothers, we have a godly heritage. Men and women of faith went before us and nurtured us. At least one other person attended our baptism. Usually we can name teachers, pastors, mentors, elders, and friends who have positively impacted our lives. We live indebted to the body of saints. Hebrews 11–12 point to the wonder of a great cloud of witnesses who labored for what we now find in front of us. These witnesses walked, prayed, lived, preached, prophesied, lost their children, and suffered martyrdom. While most of us only know a few generations of our natural forefathers, we count our spiritual heritage of faith back to Abel, Enoch, and Noah. What a heritage! Those who live by faith count Abraham as their father according to Romans 4:16.

Therefore we must stir up the gift.

We must lay aside every weight that hinders us from running well.

Practicing the spiritual discipline of stewardship requires several significant steps according to Paul's words to Timothy. First, Paul called Timothy to check his emotions. Fear serves as a signal that disciples have strayed from living in their gifts. Disciples must remember their adoption and cry out, "Abba, Father." In that moment our spirit agrees with the Spirit that we are God's children and joint heirs with Christ. (See Romans 8:14–17.) God adopted us because He sees value in us and gifts us to fulfill His purposes. Living in fear hobbles the mind and spirit; fear wastes personal and community gifts.

Second, Paul called Timothy to replace fear with power, love, and a sound mind. Disciples must have these resources if they hope to live in the place where God has positioned them in the body.

Paul's next step removes shame. Rather than seeing Timothy as living "guilty" and in need of being returned to "innocence," which might be an individualistic Western interpretation, Paul used a collectivist worldview that sees shame as the barrier. Instead of being ashamed of the Lord's message and Paul's time in prison, Timothy should embrace the difficult time he experienced on the mission. He had already received the power to do so—he just needed to use it.

Finally, Paul took Timothy to the bedrock of talent stewardship. Timothy *could* do his part in the body serving God's mission because God saved and called him with a holy calling. When students wrestle with their ability to fulfill God's purposes in their lives, I try to remind them why they received the Spirit in the first place. The Spirit and accompanying gifts come to make possible that which could not be done on our own. If we think we can do the work without the Spirit, then we either have too high an opinion of ourselves, or we have no clue of the magnitude of what God wants to do through the church in this hour. Paul gave his own calling testimony as he instructed his son in the gospel. Paul had the appointment of preacher, apostle, and teacher of the Gentiles. If Paul could hold fast through faith in the One who called him, then Timothy could do the same through the Spirit.

What gifts has the Spirit placed in your life? Remember that the giver has no "variableness, neither shadow of turning" (James 1:17). Disciples should do a 360-degree assessment. Listen to elders in your life. If those elders have already passed away, then spend a season of prayer and reflection to remember the prophecies and prayers from those men and women of faith.

Disciples gain strength in laboring together with others. Jesus always sent workers out in groups of two or more. Use peer accountability to provoke each other to righteous works and faithful stewardship of gifts (Hebrews 10:24). In addition to mentor and peer assessments, disciples should spend some time listening to those they serve.

This humbling process provides a key assessment tool in seeing how a person's gifts impact those they serve.

Finally, remember that all elements of the gift assessment process happen within the Spirit's leadership and empowering. The Spirit gifted. The Spirit will point out errors and next steps for faithfulness. Of course the whole process leads to transformation in the disciples, the body, and the mission in the world.

Personal Reflection

1. *Do a case study of your favorite biblical character or characters.*

    a. *What talents did the Lord place in their lives?*

    b. *How did they use those talents?*

    c. *Can you identify places where they matured in the use of their gifts? If so, explain.*

2. *Examine the talents in your life.*

    a. *How have you used those gifts?*

    b. *How is the Spirit calling you to develop and use those gifts for Kingdom purposes?*

    c. *Share your reflections with a spiritual brother or sister. Consider sharing the reflections with a leader in your life, a peer, and someone you lead.*

FINANCIAL STEWARDSHIP

I would be remiss to avoid the challenging topic of financial stewardship in this chapter. Even a cursory look at the biblical text demonstrates the importance God places on financial stewardship. Biblical guidance on financial stewardship serves two primary functions: (1) removing the financial idolatry of materialism and (2) underscoring God's promise to provide resources for all His children as they serve on His mission. Both prongs of financial stewardship assist disciples in pursuing a missional lifestyle.

According to a Howard Dayton article in *Leadership* magazine, Jesus used sixteen of His thirty-eight parables to talk about money and 10 percent of verses in the Gospels directly relate to money. Dayton further asserts that the Bible provides about five hundred verses on prayer while more than two thousand verses relate to money and possessions.

The Old Testament law provided strict guidelines for financial stewardship. Tithing, firstborn offerings, gleaning, weekly Sabbaths and sabbatical years, and redistribution of wealth every fifty years provide but a few examples of the meticulous attention to financial accountability under the Law. Sadly, Israel deviated from these laws as it did from the others.

The Old Testament prophets addressed financial stewardship. Many Christians gravitate to the christological prophecies of Isaiah and ignore the context surrounding those prophecies. Isaiah compared Israel to Sodom in his first chapter. Their failure to worship appropriately had driven them further from God rather than drawing them nearer. They no longer cared for the fatherless and widows; instead the princes looked more like thieves who loved gifts and sought rewards. Chapters 2 and 3 contrast the differences between God's kingdom in the last days and the condition of Isaiah's neighbors. Rather than living righteously with one another, the people had become as selfish as sinful Sodom. Rather than superintending God's abundant gifts, they abused the poor in ways that beat His "people to pieces" (Isaiah 3:15). Life revolved around pursuing wealth at the expense of others rather than living in financial stewardship.

We face several challenges in applying Old Testament law and prophecies to our contemporary setting. Perhaps the most important consideration is the way the New Testament does away with legalism. Many people lose the joy and spiritual discipline of giving because they view tithing as a legal mandate as opposed to an opportunity to bless the Kingdom. The New Testament always builds on the Law's schoolmaster rather than staying fixated on minimum standards as a way for men and women to earn right standing with God.

Jesus did not apply a one-size-fits-all approach to wealth. Rich people throwing in their whole gold-filled purses did not give as much as a widow who gave two simple coins. One rich young ruler had to face the choice of giving all to the poor as he followed his new identity in Christ or walk away in his own finely crafted identity based on personal wealth and privilege. He went away in sorrow. On the other hand, Zaccheus freely gave 50 percent of his wealth without Jesus saying a thing. The tax man no longer managed his own identity; he became a new man when Jesus crossed his threshold.

The early church functioned according to resources and need rather than a legal "tax" model of tithing as they lived out Jesus' teachings in real time. Acts 2 and

5 demonstrate the early church's commitment to generosity. Later, Paul celebrated the sacrificial offerings from the mission field that were given to care for those who suffered in Jerusalem.

A second challenge we face is the difference between an agrarian society and a capitalistic society. In an agrarian society, land exists as the source of wealth and means of production. For Israel, the land belonged to God rather than to the farmer. Israel cast lots to determine where each tribe and family would settle. Every half century, the land was supposed to revert back to those historical family allotments. Tithing served as a reminder of God's lavish benevolence as He cared for His people. Tithing only covered some of the land's produce. If we followed a legalistic approach to tithing in the church today, then I would never have to give tithes. I have no cows, sheep, wheat, or other produce.

In the West, our economy is based on a form of capitalism. Instead of land being the means of production, capital (money) takes the place of land. We say things like, "Time is money" to convey this guiding principle. In an agrarian society we would have to say, "Time is land." Rather than being a steward of a vineyard as the vinedresser Naboth, we serve as stewards of finances and the skills to generate finances. A significant challenge exists for Christians in the West today: how to provide for extended years of retirement. In an agrarian society, the land provided in old age. In a capitalistic society, investments provide security in old age. With the demise of long-term service to one employer and losses of retirement plans, Christians will have to include retirement planning in their stewardship efforts.

Finally, our conservative Christian tradition can be a hurdle in living in accordance with New Testament teaching on financial stewardship. Some readers will find challenges in approaching finances as stewards rather than as legal code followers. Perhaps remembering the faithfulness rubric will provide some help. A steward owns nothing. A steward holds his master's goods in trust to pursue the master's interest. A steward has no private property. She cannot live to give 10 percent to the owner—the owner has a claim over all! Our baptism firmly places us in the steward category rather than manager of personal wealth category. In Jesus' parable, the three stewards give all the resources back to the returning master rather than merely a tithe. The one, five, and ten talents did not belong to them to start with, so none of the increase was theirs either.

Perhaps tithing can serve as a benchmark or guideline for many even though it cannot be a legal means to earn right favor with God. In our personal lives my wife and I have always sought to give more than 10 percent of our earnings. This level of giving does not secure God's love or provide "insurance" against financial setbacks such as car breakdowns or a house burning. Sometimes the Spirit called us to give even when we had little. When He did not specify an amount, we determined how much to give as part of our joyful worship. The fluctuating amount we gave testifies to the wonder of God's provision in our lives and our commitment to use those provisions for Kingdom purposes. The years we spent paying for my three graduate degrees was a Kingdom investment in addition to our tithes and various offerings. Since the Kingdom work required me to earn additional degrees, paying for those degrees (time, money, energy, saying no to other pressing opportunities, etc.) was a Kingdom work of stewardship. At times I did not know if the costs of university were worth it; I could only trust the Teacher knew what He was doing when He called me to walk this path.

Contemporary disciples can improve their financial stewardship through a variety of practical steps. Your church might consider using Dave Ramsey's Financial Peace University program to assist the whole church. All disciples will need to focus attention on this discipline from time to time.

The following are some additional steps you can take:

1. Rededicate all of life to the lordship of Christ. Without this perspective, all subsequent steps will be financial management or wealth building rather than financial stewardship.

2. Do an initial assessment of financial status. In this step determine all expenses, income, assets, and debt.

3. Examine long-term financial concerns such as health care, retirement, elder care, providing for disabled children in their adult years, etc.

4. Celebrate the good gifts and resources the Lord has already placed at your disposal. In this stage in the process you should also remember past periods of financial faithfulness, blessings, and dark times you have overcome.

5. Repent of self-centeredness and unwarranted financial worry. Signs of sinful or unfaithful financial stewardship can be identified in the course of daily life. While a full

listing of financial stewardship shortcomings might be difficult to compile, simple indicators can include: finding value in possessions or financial assets, working just to pay the bills and stay ahead of an impending crisis, feeling unimportant or devalued due to low economic status, becoming angry when church leaders or friends talk about finances, shopping to avoid difficult situations (a.k.a. retail therapy), and saving only for personal vacations or major purchases.

6. Pray for God's direction in your life and listen for spiritual guidance. Direction for the future may relate to personal, family, and local church giftings, as well as ministry placement. All disciples need to know their place in ministry service, or they will not know how to exercise proper stewardship. Those who find themselves in this condition should take Jesus' recommendation to find supervised guidance from others until they develop the foundational skills to do so themselves. (See Matthew 25:27.)

7. Develop a triage plan to increase financial margins. While every situation will present different needs and challenges, stewards should consider these steps: reduce spending, reallocate resources, pay off debt, develop emergency funds, start or build retirement plans, and begin a fund to support your area of ministry.

8. Continue to tithe, support the church, and assist missionary efforts while you pursue financial stewardship. The Spirit will lead very few people to reduce their giving as they grow as a disciple. Of course, major life course adjustments such as going to college, having children, experiencing a health crisis, becoming unemployed, and retirement may affect giving.

9. Realize this process may take a number of years to bring about the faithfulness the Master desires for your life. Those with heavy consumer debt, academic debt, overbuilt houses, expensive hobbies, or other financial challenges must find spiritual peace in making progress rather than expecting to create financial margins for ministry overnight.

10. Determine where finances may be needed. This list provides a few examples of financial needs stewards will face.

   a. Develop skills, learn another language, pursue degrees

   b. Engage in a ministry sabbatical where you take a break from one ministry to provide space for preparing for the next season of life

   c. Conduct a missions trip (within your country or in another country)

   d. Create financial margins to care for others

11. Covenant with two or three others to review financial assessment and stewardship actions to be taken. Men and women can easily become discouraged, practice self-deception, and miss spiritual formation opportunities unless they develop accountability partners that understand the privilege of being a part of Christ's mission in the world today.

As you experience new seasons in life, you will need to adjust your financial stewardship plan to account for normal life changes, unforeseen financial crises, or external economic threats, and unexpected opportunities for ministry and financial stewardship.

RELATIONSHIPS

Perhaps Western readers only think of material things and skills when they consider resources in need of stewardship. Our Teacher, however, did not call us to serve as independent Kingdom agents. He called us to labor together with Him as He completes the work of reconciliation. As stewards we must faithfully care for our relationships as we do our spiritual gifts, talents, and financial resources.

The Harvard John F. Kennedy School of Government's understanding of social capital provides a beneficial lens for us to understand our relationship resources. "Social capital refers to the collective value of all 'social networks' [who people know] and the inclinations that arise from these networks to do things for each other ['norms of reciprocity']." In other words, our relationships provide another means of production through our daily care for one another. Collectivist societies in the biblical world and contemporary majority world value relationships as necessary ingredients for survival. Jesus taught His disciples the reality of entering a new family (social) reality when they followed His teachings. Reading through Acts and the epistles illustrates the early church's commitment to living out the gospel together. A study of Beatitudes, fruit of the Spirit, and righteousness in the biblical text highlights the premium on interpersonal relationships, as did the majority of the Ten Commandments under the Law.

The Kennedy School, as referenced above, proposes a number of ways social capital benefits its members. Groups provide formal and informal information networks. They set expectations for caring for one another. These expectations for care within the group set the stage for collective action outside of the group as well. Finally, the Kennedy School says social capital creates broader identity that helps people move beyond an individual perspective to a group perspective.

Disciples belong to a number of social groups. Stewards must care for the groups to create social capital as a divinely appointed resource. Often Christians feel manipulated and controlled by these various groups rather than taking the initiative to maximize the social capital in those groups. As explored in the faithfulness overview above, disciples accept their resources as an opportunity that comes with responsibility. Paul saw marriage and singlehood in this light when he called believers to live out their faith in their real-world circumstances. (See I Corinthians 7.) He used examples from marital status, ethnicity, and socioeconomic status (master or slave) to illustrate this reality.

When people accept the call to discipleship, they redefine every relationship. Relationships now belong to the Lord. Unmarried disciples do not live to get married—

they live to fulfill God's purposes. Their unmarried status, however, does not make them "single" in the way Western culture thinks of them. Disciples exercise stewardship of their marital status whether they are single or married. They labor with and for others. They receive care and give care. They fulfill their calling as a steward rather than living to be married or to get free from marriage.

The Harvard Kennedy School provides great application of the sociological principles of group behavior; however, they do not have the capacity to capture the Kingdom nature of discipleship social capital. Dying to self and resurrecting in Christ shifts the focus from self or one's own in-group to serving part of God's mission in the world. Abiding in covenant relationship with fellow believers frees members from squandering Kingdom resources on self or the local body of believers; instead the covenant relationship focuses efforts on being salt and light in the world and the command to make disciples. Caring for self shifts to a distant, secondary role because stewards keep the Kingdom first.

Stewards confidently trust the Master will avenge them, so they do not have to constantly pursue their own rights. Laboring together, they care for one another and feed their hungry enemies. Serving in this way provides a powerful witness to the world—a witness forged in the fires of love and suffering.

Unfaithful stewards simply bury their Master's resources and wait for Him to return. Failure to see the Kingdom potential in all relationships diverts energy and resources away from Kingdom purposes. Couples can fight over personal preferences and squander years of Kingdom faithfulness to just make a living and raise children.

Unmarried saints can fail to cherish the relationship opportunities that the Master has given them. Unfaithful stewards see the church and other relationships as places where they get served or have their needs met rather than being a dynamic, Spirit-filled component of the church living as God's mission in the world. Unfaithful stewards live in a spiritual subsistence mode just waiting for Jesus to return. They live to be served.

On the other hand, faithful stewards pursue spiritual maturity in all relationships. When they see relationships as exhausting or as a means to meet their own needs, then they repent. As they worship, God reorders all their relationships under the discipleship call. They know how to lament when relationships suffer or are lost, but they trust lament under God's care will end with an opportunity to witness God's goodness. (See Psalm 22.) Maturing disciples quickly incorporate new believers into their relationships as a means to both care for the new believer and to receive care from the Master's new gifts in the body. Faithful stewards periodically review their relationships and explore ways to pursue the Master's will in every one of them.

Personal Reflection

God's people live in relationships to both give and receive care. Begin the process of evaluating two of your core relationship groups.

   a. *What are Kingdom potentials of the group?*

   b. *How do your gifts contribute to the group and its missional faithfulness?*

> c. *How does the group call and support you as a developing disciple?*
>
> d. *How does this analysis call you to change?*
>
> e. *Consider prayers, time allocation, attitudes, and service within the group.*
>
> f. *With this in mind, start considering ways you can grow spiritually in your relationships. Remember this is a lifelong process.*

CONCLUSION

Jesus had a few things to do before He went to the cross. He had dinner with His students and washed their feet. He taught the disciples about His need to leave so He could return and take up His abode in them. He reminded them of their responsibility to continue His work in the world.

He also went to the Temple.

The Prince of Peace began to tip over tables.

Jesus demonstrated His displeasure at those who used spiritual resources for their own pleasure. Those who changed money and sold sacrificial animals found themselves avoiding the whip while chasing coins and cattle. The Teacher explained His actions by proclaiming the Temple should be a house of prayer for all nations rather than a den of thieves (Matthew 21:12–13).

The booth attendees probably experienced a little confusion at the wide-eyed anarchist in their midst. They had a right to be there. Their families had served as priests and levitical workers for many generations. If asked, they could produce family trees that went back to Aaron and even further to their tribal progenitor, Levi. They saw Jesus as the trespasser and protocol violator.

The Teacher expressed His anger because spiritual resources should be used for others rather than self-aggrandizement. They used the system to increase their power position rather than lifting up Israel and the world to God in continual sacrifice. They robbed others with their exchange rate rather than offer the priestly blessings as commanded by Moses and Aaron at God's direction. In short, the Master enacted a parable of punishing stewards who had used Kingdom resources for themselves. Jesus had taught the same principle when He told of vine dressers who killed messengers and the master's son in an effort to take over the vineyard. The Master still turns out unfaithful stewards. Fortunately, stewardship spiritual formation provides wonderful opportunities for disciples to celebrate their abundant gifts, understand the faithfulness rubric, and reorder all resources for the Master's purposes.

PRAYER

I pray you know how deeply the Master loves you and how deeply He loves the world. I pray you see and celebrate the many forms of Kingdom resources the Master has entrusted to your care. I pray you reject all words against you that cause you to feel unloved, ungifted, worthless, or incapable of Kingdom faithfulness. I pray you experience healing in your spirit, mind, and emotions that have caused you to feel empty and in constant need. I pray God's constant blessings and resources become more evident with each act of service and worship. I pray you learn to find your deepest satisfaction in faithfully exercising stewardship over the real gifts in your life now as you continue to reject daydreams and ideal worlds where you have the "perfect" place of service.

I pray you know the world awaits you and your fellow disciples' faithful service.

In Jesus' name,

Amen

10 | *Work and Leisure*

God is a worker. His first acts in Scripture demonstrate how central work is to God's own identity. The gap between the Hebrews' understanding of the relationship between God and work could not be more pronounced from that of its neighbors. Other creation stories from ancient cultures included violence between various siblings and an effort to create slaves to do the work they did not want to do. The biblical creation account explores God's personal involvement in His workshop. He spoke into the chaos and created. Everything. He created everything.

God's work schedule for that first week of the universe included quite a range of activities. God's Spirit moved across the chaos to bring creation to order. He created light and separated it from darkness. He considered His naming rights over His handiwork and decided on Day and Night. He separated water, land, and air. He named the space above Heaven. He decided He liked the name Earth for the mass beneath; the majority of this new Earth thing consisted of water. Bunches of water needed a name too; Seas would do. Creator God looked at the products in His workshop and considered the names He had chosen. In the first act of evaluation, God pronounced the results of His handiwork good. While we really cannot know what Spirit looks like when God exclaims, "It is good!" a smile of satisfaction comes to mind.

John tells us that God sent light into the world. In fact, "He was in the world, and the world was made by him, and the world knew him not" (John 1:10). Everything happening in God's workshop came from the very Word that was God. That "Word became flesh and dwelt among us" (John 1:14, NKJV). Since disciples engage in spiritual formation to be more like Christ, they must consider the spiritual formation elements of work and leisure.

IMAGE OF GOD

Work preceded human experiences of sin. God made Adam and Eve in His image and gifted them with the opportunity to continue His work in the Garden. Of course, God's creative and sustaining work never ended. His voice continued to authorize the shining of the sun and reflecting of the moon. Seas teemed with all kinds of swimming creatures. Land fed and sheltered animals from the smallest insect larva to giant beasts that still spark imagination in the minds of children and adults alike. The sky supported flights of feathered birds and winged mammals—from the falcon's diving speed of 180 miles per hour to the Brazilian free-tailed bat's horizontal speed of about one hundred miles per hour. Even today God sustains this global menagerie and pays attention to feeding those fowls of the air.

The original Worker blessed Adam and Eve and gave them the responsibility to "replenish the earth, and subdue it: and have dominion over the fish of the sea, and over the fowl of the air, and over every living thing that moveth upon the earth" (Genesis 1:28). What a job description!

Adam followed the pattern set by God and began to exercise naming rights over the creatures he cataloged.

Then sin came.

The end of Hebrews 2:8 exudes the feeling of loss we all experience: "But now we see not yet all things put under him." What had started with such hope and direct cooperation with the Worker turned into exclusion from the perfect workshop and a transition into a world devoid of such unbelievable promises. Yet the call to work continued. The consequence of rejecting God's plan included reduced productivity with every turn of the hand.

Following Adam and Eve's loss of access beyond the workshop security barrier, all relationships changed. Daily conversations with God became memories. Mutually supportive commitments to image God became seriously strained. The beauty of birthing new members to the human family produced pain. Flowers and crops suffered the choke of weeds. The first sweat drops came centuries before the first rain drops pelted Noah's single window pane.

Work suffered.

Some people work too much. Some people wait for tomorrow to work. Some people pledge never to work. Some people "retire" because the unemployment line strangled the last hope of supporting oneself and one's family. Some people get caught in the cogs of industrialization both figuratively and literally. Some people own the work of other people's hands.

What started as a wonderful collaborative venture with the Worker often sinks to mere survival or a quest to prove one's existence. Those goals grow in the same soil as weeds. Spiritual formation reclaims the human activities of work and leisure as collaboration with the Worker.

Personal Reflection

1. *How does viewing God as the Worker influence your understanding of God?*

2. *List two places in the Old Testament and two places in the New Testament where you see God as a worker.*

3. *How does God continue to be a worker in the world today?*

How Did We Get Here?

The concept of work has suffered misperceptions for a long time. A cursory study of work throughout history illustrates this in different ways: classism in ancient Greece, for example, in which work represented a lower form of living; or for another example, dualism in the Middle Ages, in which work was seen as mundane and temporary with spiritual and contemplative work belonging to a higher order. And we can see the impact of this idea of the separation of mundane work from more important work in the lives of Christians today. Saints who are in full-time ministry may be viewed as having more important work than those who work a job and do ministry "on the side" or live bivocational lives. Some Apostolics see this lower, more mundane lifestyle as inherently less spiritual than those who live as full-time ministers. They would be viewed as more spiritual if only they could have full-time church work.

Many cultures still value creative work over manual labor. Industrialization changed workers from directly producing necessities of life to earning a wage to exchange for things they need. Such work often left one feeling unfulfilled. Freud, an early-twentieth-century psychologist who still carries much influence today, believed work presented a challenge for human beings: if human beings are basically pleasure-seeking animals, then work often gets in the way. For many toilers, work became a four-letter curse word to be endured until the wonderful time of retirement allowed for more leisure.

Many middle-class women went to work with their poorer sisters after World War II. Now most women toil the extra shift by laboring both in the home for unrecognized work as well as in the public places where labor is measured in dollars. While we can celebrate the progress of equality between men and women's work, having both fathers and mothers in the wage economy creates additional stressors on home and church life. People have less time to provide the emotional needs for each other. Society's members with extra risks (e.g., children, elders, and individuals with disabilities) suffer the most due to this care deficit. Extra money can serve as a blessing at first to close the gap between expenses and income, but the toll can be high. Extra money soon becomes normal, and expected living standards change. Consequently, the two incomes struggle to keep up with the growing debt needed to cover all of the twenty-first-century "necessities."

By the end of the twentieth century, Western workers looked for work that provided a sense of self-fulfillment and satisfaction. At the same time, the hopes of increased leisure time due to mechanization of mundane tasks collapsed with the globalization of the labor market. Jobs and markets no longer stayed within national or even

continental borders. The new twenty-first-century economy often requires workers to undergo multiple career
changes across their lifetime and suffer from labor and economic anxiety with decreased job security.

Personal Reflection

1. *What work makes you feel fulfilled?*
   What work leaves you feeling unfulfilled?

2. *Now consider your work through the lens of
   discipleship. Does the unfulfilling work take on
   a new meaning when you realize the Lord calls
   you to be salt and light in all areas of your life?
   If so, how?*

THE GIFT OF WORK

While God made us in His image and gifted us with
work as a part of that legacy, work does not always seem like
a gift. Perhaps many reading this book would not go to their
current work settings next Monday if they did not need a
paycheck next Friday. A mid-twentieth-century American
psychologist, Abraham Maslow, might see work as needed
to cover the lower level hierarchy of needs so that ultimate
fulfillment or self-actualization could be experienced. We
often work to cover basic biological and safety needs; we
would be tempted not to work if we did not have to.

Discipleship calls us to reclaim this major part of life
as a gift from God and a place where we serve Him well.
Since we often feel thwarted or kept from doing things
which are important as we toil, work provides an opportunity for spiritual formation.

According to James, "Every good gift and every perfect gift comes from above, and cometh down from the Father of lights, with whom is no variableness, neither shadow of turning" (James 1:17). Even though our fallen nature brings brokenness to those gifts, the Giver has not changed His desire for the goodness and perfectness of the gift. Work provides the opportunity for both blessing and abuse.

Work as a spiritual discipline calls disciples to approach their labor as stewards of God's good gifts. While an Apostolic theology of work goes beyond the scope of this book, we can identify a number of biblical principles that influence our discipline of work. Some of those principles come from Paul's second letter to the Thessalonians.

Value work as a means to provide for ourselves. Evidently, some members of the Thessalonian congregation lived chaotic lives because they chose to accept handouts from the church's benevolence fund rather than work for their food. (See II Thessalonians 3:10–11.) It is not clear why some of the members did not work. Perhaps the church's anticipation of the Lord's soon return influenced this "why work" attitude. Maybe the cultural context in which many working-class people suffered unemployment due to the reliance on slave labor and the practice of patronage in which wealthy people economically supported a number of people forced some out of the workplace. Regardless of the cause, Paul had to strongly admonish the church to stop the practice of giving gifts to able-bodied people.

The early church practiced sharing of resources from its birth. (See Acts 2:44–47.) In fact Luke seems to imply the sharing of resources was one of the reasons the church found favor with the people. Unfortunately, churches like the one at Thessalonica had some of its saints fail in the discipline of work. They had the opportunity to work, but chose not to do so.

Walking away from God's gifts always leads to difficulty. Their unwillingness or inability to work took away resources that could have assisted the needy. Rather than being busy, they became busybodies. Finally, they developed a disorderly or chaotic way of living. In short, when able-bodied people reject God's gift of work, everyone suffers. The needy went hungry. The church experienced infighting and squandered spiritual energy that should have gone into its mission in the world. The unemployed developed erratic lives without direction.

Paul hoped his own life provided an example they could follow. Paul and his companions chose a disciplined lifestyle over chaos and disorder. Rather than taking from the church's funds, they engaged in hard labor night and day. They did full-time ministry and full-time manual labor, even though they had a right to be supported on the basis of their teaching ministry. By working, Paul lived an ordered life and paid for his own food.

The chaotic lifestyle of those who would not work represented a spiritual issue requiring physical, spiritual, and social interventions to bring about change. Paul went so far as to say the able-bodied people who did not work should not eat. He hoped hunger would motivate them to work. Social intervention included marking the person as a nonworker, excluding them from interacting with church members, and letting shame settle on them. If not working represented only an economic issue, then these measures would certainly have been too strong, but the chaotic lifestyle and busybody behaviors threatened the nonworker's spirituality, as well as that of the community. Finally, spiritual resources provided transformation for both the faithful saints and the nonworkers. When church discipline went its full course to excommunicate a person from the church, the saints had to express godly love rather than worldly animosity. By treating the shunned nonworker as a brother or sister, the church demonstrated the goal of church discipline: to restore a saint as a contributing member of the body.

Value work as a means to care for others. Paul's teaching undoubtedly brought some challenges to the church. On one hand, they lived out the faith received from the Jerusalem church by providing resources for those in need. On the other hand, Paul was telling them to express godly love by withholding food and other basic necessities from nonworking busybodies. This tension provided the context of Paul's oft-quoted dictum: "Be not weary in well doing" (II Thessalonians 3:13). While it might be difficult to withhold food from the nonworking, able-bodied believers, they should continue to do the good work of caring for those in need.

Both Paul and James called for social programs to care for the poor. Paul believed the church should evaluate the needs of widows and provide care. James identified caring for widows and children as half of the true and undefiled religion equation. As we saw above, Paul called thieves to new spiritual and social integrity. Stopping thievery did not complete the spiritual transformation process. Thieves had to change from living off of the work of others to laboring to supply their own needs and contribute to the needs of others. For an ex-thief to mature in holiness, he had to see his own life as a resource for others.

Value the provision from others when we cannot provide for ourselves. God wonderfully provides for His children. All of Scripture points to the truth that God made a world that could sustain its inhabitants. Israel's return to Canaan included guidelines for providing for the poor and the stranger. Gleaning and periodic redistribution of land guaranteed that difficult seasons of life would not relegate a segment of society to permanent lower-class status.

God gave wealth to Israel to care for both those who could labor and those who suffered. The early church celebrated their abundant resources—resources that could be shared with those who suffered want. Rather than allowing church conflict to spread because of the inequity of distribution, the church brought the problem to the apostles and ordained deacons to the task. Equitable distribution of resources served to increase the Word of God and multiply disciples. Some priests left their offices to join the church when they saw the church's faithfulness. (See Acts 6:1–7.)

Those who suffer need receive God's provision through those God has blessed with work. In essence, the gift of work to the able-bodied serves both the worker and those in need. Extra resources should not be hoarded in bigger barns. Neither should the needy reject assistance from the larger body of believers. Failure to receive when in need represents a spiritual problem as does the unwillingness to work or to share God's abundance.

Personal Reflection

1. *Reflect on your current place of work. Identify ways work provides for your own needs as well as the needs of others.*

2. *How does Paul's perspective help you see work in a more favorable light?*

3. *If you have experienced a period of unemployment or underemployment, examine the impact this had on your spirit. How might your experiences provide help for others who suffer in a global economy?*

CARING FOR THE GIFT

The split between private and public life complicates the way we think about work. This long-standing trend in the Western world places spirituality in the category of private life. Spirituality happens in the home, closets of prayer, personal Bible reading, and in church services. Work finds itself in public space, the pragmatic place of navigating social contexts. As a public and pragmatic activity, work exists primarily to provide for one's basic needs of survival and meaning.

Work, as a gift from God, calls us to recognize the spiritual nature of our labor. As stewards of the work gift we care for God's resources in us as we do in more obvious spiritual enterprises such as spiritual giftings found in I Corinthians 12 and Romans 12. Work requires us to see our labor as a means through which we serve God, not just a place where we can live out our Christian faith.

Leland Ryken provides some practical guidance for all Christians to understand their work as a vocation, a calling of God. Stewardship of God's work gifts becomes a way of life, rather than something we have to do to stay alive.

Where you are now. Many people reading this book already have a job or two, so our journey starts from that vantage point. With thanksgiving we can celebrate the opportunity to serve God and humanity in the current legitimate vocation. The primary challenge calls us to faithfully serve God and others in the job rather than seeking self-fulfillment or career development. At first glance this perspective seems impractical. Our culture tells us we have to place a priority on managing our own careers or others will outpace us. As disciples we shift from placing the priority on career to being a servant. Career development flows out of faithful service to God and others rather than self-interest and advancement. If Christ came as a servant, then we should have no fear in following His example. (See Philippians 2.) Even in situations of underemployment, a disciple will see opportunities for faithful service first rather than placing the priority on leaving that position. The disciple can labor lovingly and faithfully while looking for the next place of missionary service.

A commitment to stewardship in work requires spiritual discipline. The spiritual discipline of work will likely take time to gain appropriate attitudes and behaviors. Pride, anger, frustrations, depression, blaming others, and disappointments in our work all point to a deeper spiritual problem. These realities serve as a gift from God because they help the disciple identify the issue. Spiritual formation calls us to turn away from financial advancement, material possessions, and honor in careers to obedient service, simplicity, and humility. In moments of inner turmoil and confusion, we confess God's loving care and gifts of labor. We reorient our work as acts of service to God and others. We discover underutilized gifts that can be pressed into service. These spiritual disciplines ensure a commitment to holiness in emotions as well as labor.

(Re)Discovering a Vocational Call. If disciples do not have an awareness of their calling, or if their current calling becomes obsolete in a world of frenetic change, then they should undergo a process of discernment. This discernment process revolves around two key concepts. First, the disciple explores the potential for serving God and others in a way that lives out Kingdom principles. Some jobs provide more opportunities for service than others. Uncovering one's calling centers around receiving the call to serve. Accepting the call to serve transforms a job or career into a vocation. A second concept for one's calling comes from personal talents, interests, and abilities. Disciples know those abilities and sources of joy come from the Father above (James 1:17). These abilities and preferences should orient us toward fields of labor. Consulting with career counselors may help in finding areas where those gifts can be best utilized. Fellowship with fellow believers can reveal ways in which gifts can be utilized in different careers. Fellowship also helps us reject self-centered pursuits in our vocation.

Looking for the open and closed doors. Disciples always live on behalf of others. When we actively serve God and others through our work, we will discover strange "coincidences" of doors opening and closing. Stewardship helps the worker know God provides open doors of service. The Apostolic church understands this reality in areas of pastoral leadership. Further application of this principle helps us celebrate this truth for all saints. When disciplines quiet our emotions of pride, anger, fear, envy, and disappointment, then we can hear the Spirit's leading and see the doors being opened.

A global economy brought many changes. The days of forty years at the same factory followed by a pension are waning. People who live without vocational security may suffer anxiety and despair. Spiritual discipline in vocation provides confident anticipation of God's provision. The loss of a job may bring fear and apprehension. Disciples will choose to walk by faith rather than staying in emotional distress. When we grow through the process of spiritual formation, we learn to trust God to open and close doors, even when this process seems to take forever.

Evaluating one's job. As a young person in ministry I often heard people say that times of uneasiness meant God was preparing you to move. Unfortunately, this perspective centers on a mistaken belief that God's primary concern resides in our happiness rather than in our holy service. (See Romans 12.) Times of uneasiness certainly call us to evaluate our job and other areas of life, but God more often wants us to mature as disciples right where we are rather than move us to a new location.

If our job provides an opportunity to serve God and others as we apply our personal giftings and interests, then the job would likely be the place to stay. Across a disciple's lifespan, he or she should expect seasons of personal adjustment and recommitment. Rather than avoiding the opportunity to grow by moving to another job, spiritual formation calls the disciple to investigate the honest reasons for wanting to relocate. If the work has become boring and routine, then perhaps a renewed commitment to serving others in the job can open one's perspective to new opportunities. On the other hand, if the evaluation season of prayer, self-reflection, and purposeful fellowship with mature disciples leads to the conclusion that the job no longer provides a good place to serve God and others, then other employment opportunities should be explored. The process may lead to additional skill development and renewed passion for service and humility. The process should never lead to pride and self-vindication.

Holistic perspective—stewardship of life. Being a disciple is every Christian's primary role. All other roles revolve around this core identity. A disciple's job provides one context for development and service. Family, friendship, community, schools, and church provide additional roles. Inside each of those institutions, we face multiple role identities as well. Sometimes those roles conflict. For example, the demands of the early years of a career as an attorney or university professor war against family and church commitments. Spiritual formation helps us situate our servant identity in relationship with all other places of service. As we do so we pursue balance and peace.

Stephen Willeford, pastor of Apostolic Pentecostal Church in St. Louis, Missouri, is one of my faith heroes. His life models joyful service and anticipation of God's blessings in everything he does. At a marriage retreat, he provided a perspective of balance I find helpful in exploring the realities of role conflict. Pastor Willeford encouraged couples to see life as a journey through the Ozark mountain region of Missouri rather than the straight highways across the American plains. Instead of calculating and setting the perfect interaction between various roles, we adjust to the changing road conditions and winding realities of the journey. Early professional careers and young children create different challenges than midcareer, empty nest, and retirement. An extended health crisis or disabled family member may call for further adjustments in spiritual formation. Economic downturns such as those many North Americans faced with the housing market crash of 2008 and the following Great Recession often require role and expectation recalibration. Rural communities and urban decay present different journey conditions. When a one-bedroom condo in some major metropolitan areas can run as high as $800,000 and multiple free-standing houses in many small towns throughout the Midwest can be bought for much less than that, disciples will face different challenges.

We only have one way to negotiate the journey—we must remember we are sent into this world as reconciliation agents. (See II Corinthians 5.) Disciples who have never practiced the spiritual disciplines of work will suffer needless difficulty, and even prolonged agony, due to the misguided perspective that work life differs from spiritual life. Making the commitment to this spiritual discipline will provide a renewed joy that only comes through service. Even when feeling undervalued, being passed over for promotions, and facing arguments with coworkers or bosses, we still celebrate the wonder of God's gift of work and seek ways to better serve Him and others. (See Ephesians 6:5–11.)

Finances. Many view work as a means to make money. We should remember that the spiritual discipline of work places receiving God's gifts and serving others above finances. Disciples value work whether they receive pay, are underpaid, or enjoy an above average salary. When people equate work with the means to earn money, then unpaid care for family, people in need, or contributions to the greater good of society through volunteer work go underappreciated.

When we ascribe more value to some professions, say engineers and doctors, than we do to other professions such as schoolteachers and cooks, then we bring harm to all members of society. The spiritual discipline of work calls us to value all legitimate work. Following the example of Christ, we willingly serve the marginalized people in society even when such work does not earn the respect or remuneration that others receive. Society did not understand Jesus' care for children, the blind, and lepers; society will likely misunderstand our missionary labors in public schools, homeless shelters, and nursing homes.

We can understand why a broken world disrespects people who care for marginalized people, but we must be careful not to fall into the same trap. If a disciple rejects the call to be a teacher because of the low pay and limited community respect, then that person needs to observe whose footsteps they follow. The spiritual discipline of work allows us to reclaim the value of our own work and deeply respect the value of those who serve us.

Some vocations will make lots of money while others will barely maintain a subsistence lifestyle. Disciples with an entrepreneurial calling serve God and others by creating jobs, providing goods and services that have gone unnoticed, and using their creativity in other ways. Disciples with a call to medical healing ministry serve God and others by tending to bodies and minds just as Christ did, valuing the Creator above the creature, and bringing ethics to perhaps the largest segment of the American economy. Both entrepreneurs and physicians may be highly paid. As they practice the spiritual discipline of work, they will be good stewards of their lives and resources as gifts from God. They will not reject the financial resources, nor will they find their value in those dollars; instead they will use those resources for Kingdom purposes.

Wealthy Christians who reject the spiritual discipline of work will suffer in all areas of their lives because of the inability to serve others and the Lord and to conduct their daily business as living sacrifices. Just as surely as we will have brothers and sisters in financial need, we will have brothers and sisters in great financial abundance. Both will need care from the body of saints to mature in their specific life circumstances.

Contentment. Jesus and Paul taught their followers to place Kingdom priorities at the center of their lives. Jesus taught just as He lived: "Seek ye first the kingdom of God, and his righteousness; and all these things will be added unto you" (Matthew 6:33). The spiritual discipline of work breaks down the wall between seeking the Kingdom in church ministries and seeking the Kingdom in our work. While Jesus spent time with rabbis and doctors, he also spent time in the carpentry shop. Paul wisely instructed his younger protégé to realize that "godliness with contentment is great gain" (I Timothy 6:6).

Seeking fulfillment in work brings discontentment. In a fallen world our work brings thorns and other weeds, just as it did to our ancestor Adam. Our work life will suffer disappointments, setbacks, abuse, and even being excluded from our chosen vocation once in a while. Practicing the spiritual discipline of work helps disciples recognize their value results from belonging to the Master rather than what they do. They celebrate the gift of work as co-laboring with God as they serve others. They do not expect work to be perfect any more than they believe they are absolutely perfect. They receive grace in their labor. They find contentment.

Personal Reflection

1. *Review the steps of work reflection in this section. After a time of prayer, identify the area that caused you the most discomfort or provided the greatest opportunity for spiritual growth.*

2. *Discuss your conclusions with a spiritual friend or two.*

3. *Identify Kingdom-focused prayers and actions to guide your spiritual maturity journey in this area.*

SABBATH AND LEISURE

Contentment comes from living within Kingdom parameters. Contentment requires a celebration of these parameters. Perhaps the psalmist put it best, "The LORD is the portion of mine inheritance and of my cup: thou maintainest my lot. The lines are fallen unto me in pleasant places; yea, I have a goodly heritage" (Psalm 16:5–6). God strategically places us in positions of authority and responsibility where we can worship, care for others, and receive care. In those places we can rejoice or lament as needed.

The spiritual discipline of work requires a parallel or related discipline of rest. God rested as His last act of Creation. In the Law, God gave His servants the command to rest on the Sabbath to remember their image included the imprint of rest. Sabbath also reminded them of their freedom from Egyptian bonds. Resting well and working well go together.

Jesus confounded Jewish leaders by doing work on the Sabbath Day. He healed the sick and the blind on the Sabbath as a new sign of freedom in His kingdom. The religious rulers expressed their disapproval of Jesus' laxity toward the Law. Jesus forcefully reminded them that "The sabbath was made for man, and not man for the sabbath" before dropping the larger revelation on them: "Therefore the Son of man is Lord also of the sabbath" (Mark 2:27–28). Jesus' acts and proclamation laid claim to His identity in creation as well as recreation of humanity. Jesus called people to a form of rest that healed brokenness and made new things possible.

The author of Hebrews feared the church failed to experience this kind of rest. Rest calls us to "cease from [our] own works, as God did from His" (Hebrews 5:10). Perhaps some people believe this rest speaks of life in the Spirit; we cannot jump so quickly to this conclusion. The original audience consisted of Spirit-filled believers, yet the author issued a call to join him in laboring to enter into rest.

What happens if we do not rest well? Hebrews 4:11–12 lets us know: "Lest any man fall after the same example of unbelief. For the word of God is quick, and powerful, and sharper than any two-edged sword, piercing even to the dividing asunder of soul and spirit, and of the joints and marrow, and is a discerner of the thoughts and intents of the heart."

Without the kind of rest that reasserts creation power, we will fail to believe. Scripture itself cuts deeply into disciples to remove cancers of the soul, spirit, and heart. God gave us rest as more than cessation of work. We could define Sabbath as accepting God's invitation to join Him in an act of anarchy—the anarchy of overthrowing the Fall! In Sabbath, we live creation rest as an inbreaking reality. We learn to see the beauty of creation and recreation. We revel in the truth that we cannot achieve anything on our own. Sabbath renews our commitment to one another and to the Creator. Sabbath helps us celebrate new possibilities in our chaotic world. This discipline takes effort.

According to Jesus, the Sabbath values human flourishing rather than some rule. Rather than earning God's goodness by obeying the Law, we celebrate Sabbath because we have already received God's goodness. This discipline calls us to personal and communal accountability in delighting in God's gifts. As Norman Wirzba explains, this delight, this sheer joy is found in God's own delight in creation. God declared His creation to be very good. Rather than relegating Sabbath to a legal principle for dour existence on one day of the week, we must practice creative affirmation of God's good gifts.

In the Garden, rest was not a spiritual discipline. In Eden we would just find overwhelming delight in the smallest flower by day and the universal grandeur by each night's stargazing episode. Our conversations with each other would never have bitterness, doubt, betrayal, or shame. Certainly, sharing a cup of coffee with the Creator and a few good friends in the evening presents an image that makes our hearts laugh.

The discipline of rest calls us to live in the elements of the goodness of creation that is available to us now. Refusal to rest, to delight in something that seems to have little utilitarian value, limits us to our own vision of hope and scales back our participation in God's recreative work to what we can do alone.

Walter Brueggemann's reflections on the role of Sabbath for Israel, as well as for the New Testament church, sees the discipline as an act of resistance. In Sabbath, Israel resisted the tyranny of Pharaoh and neighboring communities. This resistance process serves as a school for our desires. By living out the spiritual discipline of Sabbath, we experience a "regular, disciplined, visible, concrete yes to the neighborly reality of the community beloved by God."

Brueggemann connects Jesus' Sermon on the Mount to Sabbath resistance. Jesus' audience wrestled with issues related to personal value, survival, and living as a different kind of people in a world in need of salt and light. To live as a sharply contrasting people, they had to resist the "natural" tendencies of the world around them just as Israel had to resist the "natural" tendency to associate life with labor and acquisition of goods. Jesus offered an alternative of seeking the kingdom of God and righteousness. (See Matthew 6.) Pursuit of the Kingdom defocused the stuff of life so they could live in accordance with the Father's good pleasure.

The spiritual discipline of Sabbath will look restrictive at times. The discipline actively says no to the god of mammon and yes to the Creator's purposes. In a fallen world, mammon seems to be in control of most people's lives—even the lives of Christians. When more of our thoughts, energies, time, and even prayers revolve around material things and worries about tomorrow, then we bow to fallen creation more than the Creator. Perhaps this reality gave birth to Brueggemann's idiom of resistance.

The spiritual discipline of Sabbath happens only when disciples begin to take steps to revolt against being controlled by circumstances around them. Disciples rebel against a wide range of "realities" such as:

- anxiety

- possessions

- idolatry of busyness

- being anesthetized by celebrity cults in sports and entertainment

- the temptation to win the good life by controlling situations and people

- being valued and respected by others more than the One we follow

- a myriad of other challenges

Where do we begin? Perhaps we start by confessing how we are enslaved by demands on our lives and have no time to rest. Just as Israel practiced Sabbath together, we will need to share the call to renewed Sabbath in our lives with others. Confess exhaustion, anxiety, tyranny of busyness, sleeplessness, emptiness, loneliness, and fear. This discipline calls us to truly believe James's admonition to "confess your faults one to another, and pray one for another, that ye may be healed. The effectual fervent prayer of a righteous man availeth much" (James 5:16). Our confession must be coupled with repentance. David's repentant prayer included a plea for a clean heart and a right spirit (Psalm 51:10). Divine healing breaks the stranglehold and wounds of mammon and related gods. Healing opens the door to the Kingdom's true essence, an essence marked by righteousness, peace, and joy in the Holy Ghost (Romans 14:17).

Do we really have a choice? While we do not want to recreate, or in some cases perpetuate, a legalistic or moralistic perspective of Sabbath, we must join together and resist all of those things which keep us from living in the rest presented in Hebrews 4. When we make this commitment, we will be ready for spiritual surgery proposed in Hebrews 4:12.

Personal Reflection

1. *From the sample list of worldly realities presented in this chapter, identify one with which you wrestle the most. How has it limited your ability to grow as a disciple, to exercise your spiritual gifts, and to rest?*

2. *Make an action plan to start discussing these realities with a spiritual friend.*

DELIGHT

Delight can begin to break through the ground as a spring crocus after a season of confession, repentance, and healing. Only when we find our delight in God rather than personal pleasure can we begin to live in Sabbath rest. Wirzba sees this part of the spiritual discipline of Sabbath as an educational task. We need reeducation to see delight in the right places. Our desire suffers from chronic busyness, belief that ceasing to work for a moment will stop all progress, relying on entertainment and addictions to help us escape, and other forms of self-abuse listed above. Some even experience boredom when frenetic busyness and new pleasures fail to bring the rush it once did.

In Sabbath rest we begin learning to think on the good, just, and praiseworthy rather than where we fall short of our fantasy world. When we resign from the ideal world of our own making, we must make a choice. To follow this discipline, one chooses to see the wonder of God's gracious gifts toward us. In short, we experience a rebirth of delight. This delight from above connects us to all of God's creation. Perhaps we could call this the ecology of delight. All of creation reminds us of God's work and rest. Sometimes we experience the reminders as a distinct herald from the throne of God; every grand-parent knows this feeling when they hold a grandchild for the first time. Sometimes the reminders sound more like an echo of grace; perhaps some of us have heard such gracious echoes when we flee from busyness and are captured by the distinct cry of an eagle or the shy glance of a fox.

Delight soon becomes a cherished gift—a gift we anticipate each day. The school of delight scrubs away anxieties of loss and uncertainties of tomorrow. According to Wirzba, this heavenly curriculum teaches us to experience and welcome each other as gifts from God. Perhaps we could go even a step further. In Christ we accept the risks involved in changing from stranger danger (*xenophobia*) to loving the stranger (*philioxenia*). Brueggemann's resistance perspective holds more truth than we like to think. Our world thrives on fear of strangers: military budgets, home security systems, border checkpoints, racial and gender wars, class envy and anger, and hoarding and protecting assets represent just a few ways we squander the blessed resources of creation.

Anyone who has worked with children for years has suffered heartbreak upon seeing a child with perpetual sadness. Life circumstances have robbed them of joy and delights of discovery the Father has placed in the child. In a similar way, our Master pleads with us to rediscover delight and joy in His goodness around us when He sees us floundering under the cares of life. Some even have left the faith because they could not replace the heaviness of life with delight that comes from being alive in Christ.

Sabbath demands resistance. It seems so impractical. We will never learn to trust Sabbath without retraining our mind and emotions. We might be able to love those who are like us, but we will never believe we can love those who despitefully use us. Without Sabbath we will never have the courage and strength to live out true loving of neighbor in this world. We will reject the wonder and complexity of incarnational mission in favor of an anemic gospel. Without Sabbath we cannot *really* live here.

Personal Reflection

1. *Identify two or three things which bring you delight. These things can include nature, art, or shared times with others. Do not include your work here.*

2. *What prevents you from seeing delight?*

3. *Pray for the courage and strength needed to join the resistance and find delight in God's many gifts around you.*

GRATITUDE/THANKSGIVING

The discipline of Sabbath offers stepping stones to living in gratitude. The world of competition, finding value in what we own, or anticipating a future season of life represent but a shadow of God's grace. By practicing Sabbath we can see and receive gifts from God and others. We can also celebrate the wonder of sharing our resources. We can see goodness all around us rather than in things we possess, control, or achieve. In Sabbath we learn to live out Paul's discipleship principle: "In every thing give thanks: for this is the will of God in Christ Jesus concerning you" (I Thessalonians 5:18).

During one painful season of my life, the Lord called me to the discipline of thanksgiving in a way I had never experienced before. Sometimes I overlook the ceaseless crashing waves of grace and fixate on the imperfections around me. The Lord offered thanksgiving as a stepping stone to renew my life. I started each day of that month with one nonnegotiable task—regardless of the day's agenda I would find something about which to give thanks. I would spend time during the afternoon or evening journaling about the wonder of that gift.

One time the workday came to an end and I still had found nothing "worthy" of thanks. As I left my office building with my head down, I spotted a small violet flower in the grass. My soul awoke. The fingernail-sized petals peeked up from beneath the shadow of the surrounding blades of grass. My heart erupted in gratitude! God had placed such a small thing of beauty in my path. My heavenly Father waited for me to see this sign of His lavish love, a love with no purpose other than to bring life and beauty. That was a good afternoon. As I strung together those thirty days of thanksgiving pearls, my soul found rest. I could breathe again.

Personal Reflection

1. *We generally give thanks for the big things in life and fail to see all of God's lavish love in the small things. Consider keeping a thanksgiving journal for a week or month as outlined above.*

2. *Give thanks.*

3. *Share your growing vision of God's gifts with a brother or sister. Consider doing a social media post on this daily journey.*

TRUST

The discipline of Sabbath requires ever more trust. Through the discipline we can learn that the Creator graciously cares for all of His handiwork. Trust's handmaiden of humility becomes our friend as well. In so-called wasteful times of Sabbath when we cease from producing, chasing, and defending, we realize our fears do not materialize as we had believed. Though fears do not have flesh and blood, they will control us unless we learn the discipline of Sabbath. It requires disciples to remove the yokes of the world, their lives, and their neighbors' lives from their own shoulders as they luxuriate in God's provision of all things.

Personal Reflection

1. *What do you fear would happen if you took a weekly period of rest?*

2. *Confess lack of trust, pride, or self-determination as needed.*

ECONOMIC AND TIME EVALUATION

Sabbath strategically places our evaluation of time and resources in the Creator's hands. Some disciples will protest they cannot afford to waste time in Sabbath disciplines. They reason the Lord will have to provide abundance before they can rest. This logic identifies at least two possible soul sicknesses. The primary sickness results from the virus of distrust as addressed above. The second sickness results from a soul that plays host to the bacteria of ceaseless consumerism. These bacteria grow well in Western cultures where identity, value, social pecking order, and happiness artificially flow from what we acquire.

The Creator offers guaranteed recovery from consumerism. Some of us do not like the medicine. Saints with acquisition and workaholic symptoms will find refreshing life in Christ only when they engage in Sabbath practices corporately. By walking together, disciples discover the value of the Teacher's life lessons. They practice applying them to their particular life circumstances. They invite spiritual peers to lovingly critique their progress. They repent when they fail. They receive forgiveness. Through fellowship, disciples break through the mundane world to the place where they see the Creator's handiwork. They walk more carefully and joyfully in the coming days.

Sometimes disciples mistake the corporate worship service as fulfilling all of their development needs. They may think the "assembling of ourselves together" is fulfilled by hearing other people teach, preach, and sing to them. Sabbath practices provide space to actually be like the first-century church by "consider[ing] one another to provoke unto love and to good works" (Hebrews 10:24). Applying apostolic doctrine doubtlessly presents a greater hurdle than hearing apostolic doctrine. We see the early church learned to live out their new life experience because "they continued steadfastly in the apostles' doctrine and fellowship, and in breaking of bread, and in prayers" (Acts 2:42). They learned to continue in the doctrine rather than simply shouting "Amen!" or clapping their hands in agreement. Noise would not help them purge the viruses of distrust and bacteria of consumerism. Living the doctrine together created a hostile environment to those diseases.

Individuals, families, and groups of fellowshiping disciples will provoke each other to evaluate barriers to Sabbath rest. All three dimensions of our lives work together to downsize our consumption and to declutter our calendars. Unfortunately, personal and family budgets cannot get fixed in one prayer meeting or Bible study. Continuous daily disciplines alone can change our lives. Sabbath provides both the goal and accountability for this kind of change.

Personal Reflection

1. *Disciples enjoy having the opportunity to be more like their Teacher. Grace and Spirit enable every step of the way. Jesus calls men and women from all situations and walks of life. In some ways a legal approach to Sabbath rest would be easier to implement than one that calls for faith. Some readers may be asking for an exact plan to follow; such a rule would require obedience rather than transformation in Christ's image. Such rules may help young children, but they would not help mature disciples. The exact plan will differ for each disciple, but the process of Sabbath rest will challenge all to trust God's provision and consistent faithfulness to advance His kingdom.*

2. *The first step is prayerfully surrendering to God's wisdom. He created both work and rest, provided the example, and invited His chosen people to follow His example. To reject the call to rest demonstrates pride and distrust. Pride presents the belief that the nonrester can achieve Jesus' character and mission by his or her own effort. Pride also wants to be known for achieving good outcomes through one's own efforts rather than resting in God's work through His body and plan.*

3. *The second step assesses restfulness in a person's life. The assessment recognizes the call to rest alongside the call to work. Modern living has*

rejected nature's way of setting a baseline rhythm. Most people do not know the rush of planting and harvesting with intervening periods of waiting. Most no longer adjust to the daylight that gives more work in the summer and more rest in the winter. We can now work around the clock and all year long. Sabbath rest goes beyond the hours needed for sleep and daily household chores. The assessment examines how much time is set aside to get away from work just like Jesus and His disciples did. If the schedule gives a whole day off without any obligations, then time will not be the issue. Most readers, however, will need to start by reserving two or three blocks of time in a week. These blocks of time should be at least three hours in length if the time must be spread across several days.

4. *If the time is not available, then strategic planning comes into play. Identify nonessential tasks and nonessential expenses. Removing tasks and expenses can free up the resources to follow after Christ in Sabbath rest. Patiently follow the identified plan until you create the margins to practice Sabbath. Maintain momentum by realizing this is God's plan for restoring all things to Himself. While not following Sabbath will not cause a person to lose his or her salvation as legalism proposes, it will hinder the ability to become more like Christ. Non-Sabbath living results in stagnant spiritual growth and ministry faithfulness as the disciple's resources become more and more depleted. Spiritual, emotional,*

and social weariness inhibit the flow of grace through the disciple to those they serve in the church, work, community, and family.

5. *Sabbath rest requires effort. Sabbath helps the disciple turn away from the near vegetative state induced by many forms of entertainment. Habits of our culture include devoting many hours to television and other media every day. Overuse of social media and sports can drain the disciple as much as getting stuck in a cycle of watching television.*

6. *Finally, include celebration of God's gifts in creation and relationships with loved ones during Sabbath times. Most disciples will need to allocate some times for quiet, alone time for rest and reflection, but they also need times for a shared meal or walk with loved ones and friends.*

CONCLUSION

Some small towns still have "blue laws" in an effort to enforce right living. City mothers and fathers restrict the sale of alcohol and close some businesses on Sundays in an effort to help people focus on being Christian. Most blue laws live only in history books. And that is where they belong. We cannot legislate trusting God to provide and to find our value in Him. Instead we have the opportunity to live out God's gifts of work and Sabbath.

Work and Sabbath spiritual disciplines reinforce our new life in Christ. Being a part of this new creation restores our identity and basic makeup in the image of God. Living in His image transforms all emotions, actions, and thoughts. Living in His image enables us to produce even greater fruit.

From time to time, disciples will need to reevaluate their living spaces and lifestyles. While having possessions does not cause disciples to sin, treasuring them does. When disciples constantly fail to find time for rest and fellowship, then busyness and cares of life threaten to choke them and drastically restrict the ability to bear fruit (Mark 4:7). Consistent frustration over lack of finances and time provides the impetus to reevaluate and practice Sabbath in new ways. Stewardship of work and Sabbath living creates margins in finances and time to find rest and spiritual renewal. By dethroning busyness, fear of strangers, consumerism, and over-reliance on entertainment, disciples regain the freedom to live in accordance with the Teacher's purposes.

PRAYER

I pray you experience the Creator's nearness in a new way as you commit work and leisure to His purposes. I pray you have the strength and courage to identify diseases in your mind, emotions, spirit, and relationships. I pray a fresh breeze of the Holy Spirit blows over those points of confession. I pray you surrender to the Word's surgery as it prepares you for true rest. I pray you accept the Lord's forgiveness when you falter on your newfound commitments to be more like Him. I pray you give support to and receive support from fellow saints as you take these significant steps of maturity together.

In Jesus' name,
Amen

11 | *Humility and Silence*

Have you ever been in a conversation with someone and realize you cannot remember the point of your discussion? At that point you have a choice to make: either you decide to value the person in front of you and attend to them, or you can continue to pay attention to something or someone else. If you choose to continue the conversation, then you should be actively present with that person. If not, then for the sake of both of you, you should say goodbye so your actions match your attitude.

To be spiritually formed in the image of Christ, we must intentionally practice the presence of Christ. We can rest assured He is present with us through the Holy Spirit, but we often must intentionally overcome barriers to being present with the Teacher. As Jesus explained in the Parable of the Sower and the Seed, we can easily let the cares of life choke out a productive relationship with Him. When we practice the presence of Christ, we choose to further prepare the soil of our lives in a way that our relationship with Him will be more fruitful.

Too often, I fail to attend to God's presence. Revisiting a couple narratives in Mark 6 can illustrate the phenomenon. Jesus had just miraculously fed the multitude with bread and fish when He ordered His disciples into the ship. Then He dismissed the crowd. Finally He went to pray alone. Mark recorded only two other crisis points when Jesus prayed alone: when He faced temptation at the beginning of His ministry, and when He had to seek strength for the Father's will to be done at the end. The crisis following the miracle bread revolved around the crowd's intent to force their kind of kingdom upon Him. The atmosphere contained a dangerous electrical charge that could spark a ministry-derailing explosion at any moment.

To summarize:

- The disciples left the miracle bread and headed into a storm.

- They failed to understand the bread because of their hardened heart.

- They could not recognize Jesus as He walked on the waves.

The disciples missed an opportunity to see Jesus' glory in a new dimension as He "passed by" because they wasted the miracle of the bread. They could not grasp the kind of king Jesus came to be. He refused national acclaim and ethnic fervor. He came to suffer so that all creation could be restored. The disciples were unable to be present with Jesus; they could only marvel at His ability to calm the sea.

Personal Reflection

Reflect on a crisis moment when you failed to attend to Jesus' presence.

    a. *What held your attention instead of the Master?*

    b. *Why was that more captivating than Jesus' assurance that He was near?*

    c. *What can you learn from that experience to help you recognize Jesus' nearness now and in the future?*

EYES TO SEE AND EARS TO HEAR

Jesus still looks for a church that has eyes to see and ears to hear. Spiritual formation will generally not include prayers for God to speak, for He constantly desires communication with His people. The problem is not getting God's attention. The problem is giving God our attention. We do not need Him to start speaking—we need to start listening.

Jesus' coming included continuities with God's care for His people in the Old Testament as well as new and startling discontinuities. Spirit and Word demonstrated their power in Genesis 1 as well as the opening chapters of each of the Gospels. Jesus' ministry had many parallels with Moses, as promised in Deuteronomy 18:18. Jesus came to bring deliverance. He spoke the Law in a new way. He fed the people with miracle bread in the wilderness. John's Gospel made the connections clear with the first sign of changing water into wine in place of the plague that changed water into blood. Similarly, in the last sign Jesus reversed the power of death by calling Lazarus from the tomb in place of the angel bringing death to first-born children across Egypt in the Book of Exodus.

John's Gospel began with a declaration of the differences between Moses and Jesus. Law's grace could only be given by Moses, but grace and truth came by Jesus (John 1:16). The difference rested in grace and truth personified rather than the change from law to grace. The Law was gracious—every invitation to relationship with God exudes grace. In Jesus, however, grace could be heard, seen, and handled (I John 1:1).

Jesus' healing of a blind man in John 9 provided evidence that a new thing had begun. This kind of miracle powerfully demonstrated that Jesus came to give light and understanding to a dark world. Light came into the eye as well as into stale constraints that robbed people of precious gifts from God. Law without light blinds and shackles. Jesus brought light and liberty. No one could remember a story where someone had opened blind eyes in the past (John 9:32).

Jesus still wants to open the eyes of the blind today. As excited as we are when we hear of such a miracle in the physical, an even greater miracle happens when we allow ourselves to see Jesus' work through eyes of faith. While everyone argued about the blind man's ability to see in John 9, the real burst of sight happened at the end of the chapter when the man asked to know the Son of God. Jesus linked the ability to see and hear in His response: "Thou hast both seen him, and it is he that talketh with thee." The man responded as we all must: he believed and worshiped Jesus.

We have good company when it comes to our dullness of hearing. Jesus' words to the seven Asia Minor churches included an invitation to hear what the Spirit was saying to the churches. The church needed to respond to the Spirit's voice rather than ask for the Spirit to speak. The Spirit spoke specific words of commendation and condemnation and offered promises to the overcomers that connected to their individual churches. Jesus also invited the churches to hear the Spirit's words to other churches. We still get to "eavesdrop" on the Spirit's conversation with those churches.

Disciples today have the same opportunities. The Spirit still speaks to us personally, as a local congregation, and to other churches. Capitalizing on this opportunity requires a commitment to practice Jesus' presence every day. While Jesus still occasionally blinds someone with insight who is simply going about his or her daily business as He did with Saul in Acts 9, He usually waits for the blind to acknowledge His presence and ask to see. Being aware of Jesus' presence allows us to hear His invitation: "What wilt thou that I shall do unto thee?" Our wisest response would be like the blind man who heard that Jesus passed by his corner: "Lord, that I may receive my sight." (See Luke 18:35–43.)

All disciples will need seasons of spiritual formation when they deeply quest for Jesus' sight-bringing presence. These disciplines make "praying without ceasing" and asking for "Thy kingdom come, Thy will be done" a more natural occurrence.

The first step in the process involves recognizing our blindness. Much reality happens outside of our field of vision. Often, we resemble a thirsty person crawling toward a cruel mirage in the desert rather than deeply drinking from the water of life. Drinking of eternal water places artesian wells within the mature disciple. (See John 4:10–15.)

The second step orients the disciple toward the only source of life. When one learns to value the presence of Christ,[1] then all other sources of joy, satisfaction, and hope take their appropriate place behind the One who calls us. This step enables the disciple to attend to Christ's presence, to actually live like He is a constant companion. As with other spiritual disciplines, practicing the presence of Christ should happen in individuals as well as in church community life. For example, just as believers should start their day with an acknowledgment of Jesus' presence and direction for the day, every church business or planning committee should begin with attending to the One who truly calls the meeting to order. Orienting prayer and Scripture study enables committee members to realize the One who provides the analysis and inspiration needed for ministry plans. We do not want to contemplate the alternative.

The third step is to live every part of the day as an act of service to Christ. Caring for family members, nailing shingles on the roof, conducting a financial audit, and spending time on the city bus all become the context for hearing and seeing the work of the Spirit. Worship no longer gets segregated or compartmentalized to Sunday morning. All of life becomes the stage to hear and respond to the Spirit.

Fourth, celebrate the time spent attending to Christ's presence and listening to the Spirit. As stated above, He is always present and always speaking, so we do not need to find some magical way to get God to show up. Instead we can reflect on the amount of time we are aware of His nearness. How does Christ's presence change the way we work, rest, travel, eat pizza, or practice a musical instrument? How do moments of frustration or daydreaming highlight moments when we ignore the One who gives us life?

Fifth, repent and accept Jesus' continued presence when you find you have avoided Him for a portion of the day. Do not give up. He has not gone away, even when you recognize you have ignored His voice. In this case, repentance looks to bring change rather than a feeling of failure or extended sadness for not listening to Jesus. Learn the joy of growing. Practicing Christ's presence requires discipleship formation over an extended season rather than a Monday morning commitment to be different.

Finally, put growth points into practice. Similar to human friendships, practicing the presence of Christ enables us to learn the subtle cues in our relationships. Repeat behaviors that help you focus on Christ; lay aside the weights that easily beset you. Serving others, eating bread, feeling the sun, drinking water, and so many other common activities become holy when we recognize Christ is always with us. Look forward to the next fellowship or committee meeting as a time when brothers and sisters will demonstrate their commitment to live with eyes that see and ears that hear.

Personal Reflection

Every reader of this book has a weekly spiritual rhythm. Think back over your last week. When were you aware of Jesus' presence? At what points did you live without being aware of His nearness?

    a. *Consider charting awareness on a scale of one to ten for the major periods of each day of the week.*

    b. *Celebrate moments when you know He was near. Give thanks for those moments.*

    c. *Identify one or two repeating activities where you do not listen for Christ's presence. In prayer commit to being present with Christ during those times.*

    d. *Seek long-term change in the areas where you do not recognize Christ's presence. Let His presence become more real even during times of work around the house or on the job.*

    e. *Don't be surprised when Jesus radically grabs your attention in mundane parts of life as you seek His presence.*

HUMILITY

Many biblical scholars consider James's epistle to be the New Testament's contribution to wisdom literature. The apostle wrote the letter to strengthen his scattered congregation. From the opening of the letter, James called the saints to carefully attend to how they interpreted events around them. News had reached back to Jerusalem that many saints experienced suffering and were tempted to turn back on the walk of faith. James encouraged them to reframe temptation and struggles as the context for joy rather than despair. Staying faithful would bring patience and maturity in the saints. The remainder of this ancient letter helps us to understand this way of faith does not happen without a commitment to living out one's faith.

Many failed. Failures included failing to live out the Word, classism, backbiting, cursing, and bitterness. Perhaps the downward spiral bottomed out at the beginning of chapter 4 where Pastor James explained that church wars and lusts prevented them from having their prayers answered. Perhaps they too risked losing their candlestick as did the church at Ephesus (Revelation 3:5).

Fortunately, God never leaves us alone, even when we persistently miss the target.

James offered hope to the saints who still listened as their house church leaders read the rest of the letter. "But He giveth more grace. Wherefore he saith, God resisteth the proud, but giveth grace unto the humble. Submit yourselves therefore to God" (James 4:6–7). The pastor suggested grace would work on behalf of the proud and for the humble. Proud disciples will experience God's presence as resistance, while the humble will bask in grace's embrace once again. The proud will continue to harden their hearts as they elevate their right to self-govern over that of God's lordship. On the other hand, the humble surrender to God's will.

Practicing the presence of Christ makes following God's will a daily task rather than the kind of "big will of God" questions when we wonder where to live or which career path to follow. While those issues do relate to God's will, the day by day, actually moment by moment, attending to God's will is the place where we position ourselves in grace's epicenter.

Some church traditions use sacramental language to discuss the place where grace meets humanity. We believe baptism is sacramental because something happens at baptism. We receive remission of sins—a significant grace moment. Practicing humility is one such sacramental moment. Submitting to God, and recognizing we need Him, places us in the position of receiving grace. Of course in doing so we resist the devil. Drawing near to God effectively banishes the enemy of our soul. Who would not want humility?

Humility can be simply understood as seeing oneself in proper perspective with God and others. While false humility destroys the value of a child of God by seeing no value in one's life, true humility finds value in submission to God and each other. Humility does not see oneself above or beneath the value of any other person.

In I Peter 5:5, Peter quoted the Old Testament and linked mutual submission in the body to being submitted to God. As we place ourselves appropriately in relationship with one another we will find the "clothing of humility" starts to fit us more and more. Biblical humility includes recognizing our need for God and other people. Pride deludes weak disciples into thinking they are self-sufficient.

Humility is not a virtue in our world any more than it was a virtue in the Greek and Roman world. The opposite is *wisdom* in our world—self-sufficiency and self-esteem become life goals. The very idea is laughable! Many people do not know what to do with themselves if they misplace their phone or lose internet connection for half a day. Globalization helps us accept the reality that our daily existence requires the heavy lifting of a global economy. Our shirt might be from Korea or Pakistan, shoes from China or India, belt from Brazil, car from Japan or Germany, and oil from Oklahoma or the Middle East. This wide variety of global influences guarantees that no one even begins to approach self-sufficiency.

Practicing God's presence allows us to fully experience our humanity. Such humility positions us under the "mighty hand of God" (I Peter 5:6). During multiple points of this spiritual exercise, disciples will have to face their anxieties. What happens if I am not in control? When will I be hurt again by someone who misuses submission in the body? How do I trust people in such an angry and violent world? Where does God go when I feel so alone?

God goes nowhere. He never leaves.

Instead He invites us to cast all of those anxieties on Him (I Peter 5:7). As Peter explains, not giving our anxieties to God comes from our pride, our desire to walk alone. We should accept Pastor Peter's admonition to remain vigilant if we wish to stay out of the adversary's teeth.

As we read James and Peter we realize we will have challenges and disappointments in this world. These challenges can reinforce our need for God and His people if we practice Christ's presence in humility. The only other option is to desperately cling to our anxieties and try to throw off our crosses. Keep the cross. Surrender the anxiety to His loving care. Be healed by Christ's presence. Such healing comes through laying on of hands, confession, and the fervent prayer of righteous men and women. (See James 5.) Say goodbye to the unspoken requests. Name the pain or sorrow. Call an elder. Confess to a brother or sister. Pray together. Recognize Jesus is already there speaking peace, hope, and purpose in spite of the storm.

Can you hear? Can you see?

Personal Reflection

1. *The myth of being self-sufficient and independent feeds a prideful spirit.*
   a. *When do you feel less valuable than someone else? When do you feel more valuable than someone else?*

   b. *Confess your answers to another believer and seek right relationship with God through repenting of pride or false humility.*

2. *Identify current anxiety issues in your life. Being humble casts off these anxieties.*
   a. *What steps of humility can you take in prayer, rest, or serving others to let God have your anxieties?*

3. *Think about the differences between carrying your cross and carrying your anxiety. Name some of the crosses you carry. Repent of your efforts to get them off of your shoulder. Commit to joyfully living with the cross and casting the fears or anxieties on Christ. As with all spiritual formation, give yourself time to develop the spirit of humility.*

IF THE LORD WILL . . .

James 4 takes us to another key element of practicing the presence of Christ. We should find great comfort in knowing the author and finisher of our faith surrounds us at all times. Frenetic change causes us to lose our way on regular occasions, but we know the One who holds yesterday, today, and tomorrow in His hands. We do not know what will happen tomorrow, but Emmanuel, God with us, always does.

Some readers may hear echoes of the past when an elder would say something like, "I'll see you on Saturday, Lord willin'." Perhaps such sentiments seem less sophisticated, whimsical, or even juvenile. James thought otherwise. He believed the humility of holding loosely to all things in life offered the only lifeline from the cesspool of self-centeredness. The idolatry of self-centeredness requires the sacrifice of our humanity as we devalue others and reject the continual presence of God in our lives. Such boasting certainly declares empty bravado at best. Baser forms include wars brought on by unfulfilled lusts and friendship with the world as outlined by James at the beginning of the chapter.

It does not have to be this way. Jesus is present. Let Him touch your eyes and your ears.

Living in Christ's presence frees us to place all of our plans in His hands. If He wills, then today and tomorrow's plans can develop. If not, then we can surrender to His gracious care both to meet unseen needs and to give us the courage to walk through new doors of ministry service.

Perhaps an action item might begin with looking at your calendar and intermediate-term plans with the present Christ and a maturing disciple. Consider asking some of these questions:

- ✓ Do you feel like you do not have enough time or end each week with emotional, spiritual, physical, and mental exhaustion?

- ✓ Which calendar items and intermediate plans pursue things that may be good but not necessary? For the purpose of this question consider using the eternal principles of faith, hope, and love as evaluation tools. If something does not have eternal consequences, then it might be a needless drain on resources of time, money, and energy.

✓ Can you cut away or adjust some plans in a way that better reflects Christ's presence? Listen to the Spirt. Pray for your eyes to be opened.

✓ What anxieties do you face as you conduct this exercise? Do you have the courage to cast those anxieties on Christ or do you carry them alone?

Lord willing, you can reduce the stress on your calendar and emotions. The present Christ wants to provide healing. Is that something you need?

Revolutionary Silence

Pause for just a moment. What noises in the room exist at the fringes of your attention? What sights and smells exist in the room that you do not even notice any more? What did you have for lunch yesterday? What deep, soul-enveloping joy did you experience last week? What are some of those so very important things that you have trouble remembering? When did you get bored last? How do you respond when a child struggles in finding the words to tell you a story?

We live in a noisy and busy world. Often people call this a rat race, though I believe this would demean those little rodents. Resigning to live in a frenetic pace attacks the image of God in disciples. Seasons of rest in times of leisure, as discussed in the last chapter, provide a significant part of the answer. Occasional media fasts can help to quiet the noise as well. Practicing silence helps disciples draw closer to Jesus in times when they feel overwhelmed or when they prepare for a new challenge.

An examination of Psalm 46 helps God's people honestly acknowledge a number of realities, see the end of history, and still their inner storms to know God indeed is God. The psalm's three parts provide concrete instructions for practicing Christ's presence when chaos seems to win or in times when the race has left us completely depleted and without any feeling. The discipline of revolutionary silence provides the place for disciples to hit a reset button. The discipline works best when a person desires to experience Christ's presence enough to completely unplug from the world around him or her. Revolutionary silence begins to be effective with a minimum of three or four hours, but soul-cracking dryness may require multiple days of being alone with Christ.

Part 1 of Psalm 46, verses 1–3, calls for confession. Silence provides a place to confess God's help in trouble, the believer's commitment to muzzle the fangs of fear, and naming the forms of confidence-shattering disorientations that surround the believer. God has and always will be present as refuge and strength; that will never change. Unfortunately, seasons of ongoing storms can rattle confidence in God's goodness in one's specific set of circumstances. Notice the layers of destruction the psalmist forces the reader to see:

- Earthquakes—earth be removed and the mountains carried into the sea

- Hurricanes—waters roar and are troubled

- Volcanoes—mountains shake

And these are just signs of devastation in the physical world. What sources of destruction exist in the spiritual world around us?

Part 2 of the psalm, verses 4–7, records appropriate evaluations of events. The psalmist declares God's work in times of disorder. God is present even when earthquakes, hurricanes, and volcanoes rock our world. God's rivers and streams engulf His abiding place with blessings. When we dare turn our backs on the din of the storm in revolutionary silence, we will eventually see both the water and the river of life. Such sight rarely happens in a moment or even in one "sweet hour of prayer." Rebuking the storms in silence lets the disciple experience the small voice as did the prophet Elijah. Neither the assault of Jezebel nor the fire-charred mountain spoke the truth; only the voice did (I Kings 19:12).

Are we willing to take the risk to silence all around us? Maybe that is why most people fear the discipline of revolutionary silence. Silence will make us confess a couple of things: we only feel at home in the noise, and we are afraid the voice will not meet us.

The psalmist encourages us to hold to the silence until we know God is present, we will not be moved by the chaos, and God will help us. God does some of His greatest work in the chaotic times. (See Genesis 1.)

God's presence exists for both His people and the world ordered against Him. The heathen rage against God as the earth heaves with pain. Kingdoms convulse. The earth melts. If a disciple stays in a silent place even when nations topple and economies crumble, then he or she can know: "The Lord of hosts is with us; the God of Jacob is our refuge. Selah" (Psalm 46:7).

The concluding part of the psalm, verses 8–11, holds a final promise for those who stand still when everything else crumbles. They will witness God's handiwork—His desolations. Usually desolation speaks to wasted land. A paradox awaits those who risk revolutionary silence—they will see broken bows, spears, and chariots as the Creator enforces a final peace. All war will end. All storms will pass. The land stands still for those who will "be still, and know that I am God: I will be exalted among the heathen, I will be exalted in the earth. The LORD of hosts is with us; the God of Jacob is our refuge. Selah" (Psalm 46:10–11).

Practicing revolutionary silence requires a commitment, as does prayer, Bible reading, and loving service to others. Being still when everything moves around the disciple draws on reserves of faith. In those moments the disciple does nothing. In nothingness God can be heard.

The nothingness of revolutionary silence does not make God speak any more than prayer does. God always speaks. Silence enables the disciple to experience the vertigo of total chaos on the way to a new dependence on Christ's presence.

I wish silence came easily. Instead, revolutionary silence exposes deep frustrations, anxieties, and dimensions of pain or discomfort that have gone unnoticed for a long time. Early practitioners of silence will reach for phones, itch for the internet, fear what they may be missing, and breathe powerlessness that comes from inactivity.

Why would anyone want to experience such difficulty in complete powerlessness? Simply put, when we are weak, the Teacher is strong.

He has always been strong.

He has always been near.

Silence helps us know His closeness again.

Trust the ever-present Christ to be with you as you practice the psalmist's call to silence in God's presence. While Christians may be more comfortable with the "joyful noise" components of our spiritual life, we can also learn the sweetness of being silent in His presence. Start with small blocks of time if you need to. The discipline will make you more comfortable the more you are alone with Him. He has been speaking; let Him heal your ears so you can hear.

In recognition of the difficulty of accepting revolutionary silence, disciples might find the following steps to be helpful:

1. Start small by turning off radios and media while traveling.

2. Turn off cell phones at the end of each day.

3. Make an appointment in your calendar to be alone with God for three to five hours. The appointment cannot happen at home, work, church, or any other place where you take care of business. A place in a deserted park or woods will do if available. Leave phones, cameras, and all digital devices at home. Take only a Bible, journal, and writing supplies.

4. Set no agenda other than being alone with God. Make your prayer a promise to simply be

present with God and to listen for His voice. Ask for His grace to help you in the process.

5. Sit still.

6. Actively resist all problem solving and to-do items as you mentally disengage from your daily routines.

7. Listen for the Spirit. This listening will include Scriptures the Spirit brings to your remembrance.

8. Give yourself permission to feel any emotion you experience.

9. Expect cycles of thankfulness, listlessness, loneliness, etc.

10. Write down or draw pictures in the journal to capture emotions, Scriptures, and spiritual insights that you hear.

11. Repeat.

12. Expand this exercise to a day or two after you have grown proficient in the shorter periods of silence.

CONCLUSION

God created us to be in perfect communion with Him. Sin broke the ability to be present with the Creator in that way. Being born again of water and Spirit places us back in that relationship. The spiritual formation of practicing the presence of Christ prepares the disciple to hear the Spirit's continual speaking.

Practicing the presence of Christ requires disciples to pay attention to His voice above all other voices. In addition to the disciplines of humility and revolutionary silence as outlined above, you might consider one of the following disciplines to assist you in refocusing on the ever-present Christ.

- Consciously speak to the Lord throughout the day. Just as you may do with a dear friend, spouse, or child, speak to Jesus to let Him know you are aware of His nearness. Adopt words that have meaning for you. You could say something like, "Jesus, I know you are with me at all times." "I surrender this moment to you, Lord Jesus." "Guide my steps this moment by Your Spirit and Your Word."

- Realize all of creation already practices the presence of Christ. The heavens declare His glory. (See Psalm 19:1; 50:6.) He has intimate knowledge of every bird. One way you can do this is to intentionally attend to the presence of Christ every time you see the sky, feel the sun, or experience rain or snow falling.

- Israel practiced the presence of the Lord by attending to His oneness every time they went through a door. (See Deuteronomy 6.) Each time you leave your house, pray God's purposes on the journey. Each time you enter a door of business, work, or entertainment, pray for God's provision and blessings on those you encounter. When you return home, pray a prayer of thanksgiving for your home that serves as a Kingdom embassy in your neighborhood.

- Meals and cups of coffee become special when shared with a friend. Rather than eating and drinking as quickly as possible, make mealtimes or coffee breaks opportunities to remember Christ's nearness and desire for communion with you. Bread and grapes naturally connect to the Lord's Supper, but any meal can provide for open eyes when we realize Christ is present. It happened in Emmaus; it can happen again. (See Luke 24.)

- Make acts of service for family or others an act of service you do with the Lord. Even the small tasks of feeding a child or elder can be done in Jesus' name and unto Him. (See Matthew 25.)

- See people and crowds as mission fields. You will pray without ceasing as you intercede on behalf of those you encounter in bustling traffic, competitive workplaces, and hurried supermarkets.

Personal Reflection

1. *How did this chapter make you feel?*

2. *Reflect back on your week. What are some naturally occurring moments that you could intentionally practice the presence of Christ?*

PRAYER

I pray you have the courage to rebel against the noise of life and begin the process of celebrating the presence of Christ in a new dimension. I pray the Holy Spirit in you brings healing to your ears so that His voice gains priority over all other voices. I pray you persevere through the temporary disappointment that comes in learning to observe Christ's presence in times of silence. I pray you trust He is doing the work when you feel powerless to address the emotions that arise when you can do nothing. I pray you begin to see Him afresh through the tears that will come . . . or through the absolute dryness that empties every cell of your body.

I pray you look for the presence of Christ in absolutely every part of your life. I pray abiding in that awareness takes precedence over every other priority. I pray you find ways to share that awareness with others.

In Jesus' name,

Amen

12 | *Loss and Suffering*

Accepting Jesus' offer to follow Him includes an invitation to follow Him completely. After Jesus fed the multitude, He began to teach the principles behind multiplying the bread. He wanted to be the bread of life for all who had tasted the miracle that day. Once Jesus began speaking about eating the bread, the multitude faded away. I do not know if we can infer Jesus' feelings from the words He spoke to the Twelve or not, but they sound a little melancholy to me. He asked them a pointed question, "Will ye also go away?" Peter answered for the group, "Lord, to whom shall we go? Thou hast the words of eternal life." (See John 6:66–68.)

Following Jesus includes so many wonderful miracles and possibilities that did not exist when we walked our own path. Following Jesus may also include times of suffering and brokenness. Jesus offers abundant life while also demanding taking up a cross and following Him. Peter's confession at Caesarea Philippi holds such wonderful truth: Jesus is "the Christ, the Son of the living God" (Matthew 16:16). Yet Peter could go from such divine understanding to uttering Satan's perspective a few verses later when he rejected Jesus' words concerning the Crucifixion.

Spiritual formation calls us to hold these realities together. We have abundant life, and we die daily. Excarnational discipleship works hard to get us out of difficult situations. Incarnational discipleship looks for the purposes of God to be fulfilled in times of blessing and difficulty.

An examination of spiritual formation in times of suffering and broken dreams will center around living the baptized life, as discussed in chapter 4. If we are indeed a new creation in the resurrected Christ, then the Lord draws our boundaries in pleasant places (Psalm 16:6). Our situation becomes bearable when we recognize that the Teacher continues to walk with us in those circumstances. Holiness calls us to embrace times of suffering along with times of blessing as Paul did in II Corinthians 12:10. This chapter examines biblical and theological elements of spiritual formation in suffering. I will include personal illustrations related to the broken dream of ministry calling and a long-term illness.

Personal Reflection

1. *What is your view of suffering? Write out your definition of suffering for further reflection at the end of the chapter.*
2. *How do you pray during challenging times?*

LIVING AS WORSHIPERS

More and more Christians see the benefit of worshiping God in all areas of life rather than just the "music set" on Sunday morning. Worshipers live out baptized reality at home and work in addition to times of gathered worship.

Spiritual formation in times of suffering challenges the worshiper's identity and value. Worship transforms the worshiper by placing God above the crises.

Perhaps a good place to start is with the One being worshiped. The author of Hebrews provides a conclusion for all of the work in his first seven chapters by stating, "We have such an high priest, who is set on the right hand of the throne of the Majesty in heavens; a minister of the sanctuary. . . . For every high priest is ordained to offer gifts and sacrifices: wherefore it is of necessity that this man have somewhat also to offer" (Hebrews 8:1–3).

The opportunity to encounter God both in daily life and gathered worship has its beginning in divine invitation. We do not welcome God in worship; instead Jesus welcomes us into worship. Jesus serves as worship leader in all life situations. He has the capacity to do so because He has experienced the human condition. (See Hebrews 4:14–16.)

The apostle Peter initially rejected the invitation to suffer when he thought others might escape similar circumstances. When Jesus reiterated His invitation to Peter to follow Him (John 21:19), Peter wondered if John, the beloved disciple, would have to glorify God in death just as he would. Jesus basically told Peter that was not his business. Over the course of Peter's spiritual formation, he reached a different understanding of suffering. By the time he wrote his first epistle, Peter saw the way Jesus identified with us in suffering. He also stated we have the opportunity to identify with Jesus in our suffering. (See I Peter 2:21; 4:1.)

Peter saw suffering as an opportunity to live out Christ in our lives. The process from I Peter 3:14–16 includes holiness in our hearts and readiness in our minds.

Suffering reveals what is in our hearts.

In August 2014 I had the opportunity to know Jesus in a new dimension. Over a period of three days I went from being in my office as dean at Urshan College and Urshan Graduate School of Theology to the critical care unit of a local hospital where I experienced a progressive paralysis over much of my body. After a couple days, the Miller-Fisher syndrome diagnosis came back positive. My body's immune system began attacking a part of my nervous system. The nausea and pain inhibited my ability to think and maintain spiritual balance. Enduring each moment required focused effort.

Suffering revealed what was in my heart. Life changed as I knew it.

Over the course of the ensuing ten days in the hospital and five months of recovery, a series of choices relentlessly claimed my attention. Though I had been a disciple for the vast majority of my life and a credentialed UPCI minister for thirty-four years, I still faced a choice: treat the illness as spiritual formation or walk away from faith. While others may face different choices, here are the crossroads the Lord invited me to navigate in that season of spiritual formation. I could:

1. Feel betrayed

2. Lose faith and backslide

3. Live in anger beyond the temporary response

4. Die inside and just try to be saved

5. Envy the blessings of others

6. Seek to get even

7. Constantly focus on answering life's big questions

8. Look for ways to deaden the pain

Fortunately, I did not face these situations on my own. Christ stayed with me. The Spirit aided me as I made the right choice in each dimension of my faith crisis.

Personal Reflection

1. *Write out your definition of worship.*

2. *How can you broaden the contexts of worship to include both glorious and suffering circumstances?*

3. *What choices did you make in suffering seasons in the past? How did those choices control your emotions and spirit more than the circumstance itself?*

4. *Carefully consider spiritual choices in front of you right now. These spiritual choices develop in all seasons of life. How might these choices set you up to successfully navigate your next crisis situation?*

SUFFICIENT GRACE

Suffering provides the opportunity to see God's lavish love if we willingly pay attention to His nearness. During my prolonged season of illness, the Teacher showed me His love on a regular basis. The lavish love started even before I suffered the illness.

During the summer of 2014, my Sunday school teacher at the Sanctuary UPC in Hazelwood, Missouri, walked us through II Corinthians. I dutifully took notes as I always do. I wrote the lesson outline in one color of ink and my questions, comments, and reflections in another color. I looked forward to using the information to help others in my teaching and preaching. The Teacher had a different reason for that Sunday school class. Robin Johnston, UPCI editor in chief and adjunct professor of historical theology at UGST, enabled me to see Paul's trial—a trial that helped Paul hear God's voice. The Lord told Paul, "My grace is sufficient for thee: for my strength is made perfect in weakness" (II Corinthians 12:9).

As the illness took over all areas of my life, that gift from the Teacher ordered my thoughts. I knew hundreds if not thousands of people joined me in seeking a miraculous recovery. Within a couple weeks I began to learn the meaning of sufficient grace. The school of suffering teaches us to privilege God's grace over our own wishes. While I initially wanted healing, I learned to cherish God's grace even more.

Then my life changed one more time. The Visitor made His way to my room without triggering security alarms. My Visitor never experienced trouble with locked doors and barred windows before; why would He have any trouble getting past critical care security staff? My Visitor came when I was alone. He stood at the foot of my bed. He wore white. He brought a white wheelchair with Him. Somehow His face showed both loving concern and gentle peace. He spoke.

"Son, if you will get into my wheelchair, I'll take you wherever I need you to go."

In the vision I replied, "Okay, I'll sit in the chair as a little boy with innocent faith. Dad always said you would never turn away childlike faith."

Jesus' gentle response startled me, "No, son, I won't let you sit in my chair if you come as a little boy."

Confusion wandered through my mind and spirit. "Well, I guess I'll come as a young man. I had such vision, passion, and strength for ministry back then."

Strike two. "No, son, I'll not take you like that either."

Was my response frustration, resignation, or despair? As a professor with three graduate degrees, I am generally pretty good at taking tests. Thirty-plus years of ministry failed to provide the key to getting out of bed and into Jesus' chair.

I decided to try the only option I had left. "Well, I guess I'll come as a broken-down fifty-two-year-old man that can't speak, read, walk, or do anything of value. I have nothing else left to offer."

Was it a smile or just the Visitor's microexpression that telegraphed I had finally stumbled on the right answer?

"If you will come like that," the Visitor replied, "then I will push you wherever I need you to go."

How such gentle words could give me the courage to trust Him I will never know, but my life had changed for the second time in four days.

Even though a multitude of people prayed for my healing during those days, even though I fully believed God could miraculously help me walk out of the hospital, the Visitor had a better plan. Riding in Jesus' wheelchair took me the long way home.

Personal Reflection

1. *Read II Corinthians 12:1–11. Record your reflections on Paul's experiences.*

2. *Now consider a time when God did not answer your prayer in the way you thought He should have.*

   a. *What can you learn about God's sufficient grace in your experience?*

3. *If you are going through a period of suffering now, pause and write out a prayer for God's grace that can guide you through this valley of the shadow of death.*

   a. *Pause again and experience the reassuring presence of the Holy Spirit.*

CHOOSING FAITH

Spiritual formation in suffering calls for ongoing faith choices. Suffering places one's faith under a microscope to see where we can "present [our] bodies a living sacrifice, holy, acceptable unto God, which is [our] reasonable service" (Romans 12:1). Choosing faith provides wonderful worship opportunities. Sometimes those opportunities happen quickly, but sometimes they can take decades.

The teenage shepherd boy must have wondered about the meaning of the anointing as he meandered his way through the canyons to round up his sheep. Standing before the famous aged prophet inspired awe, but the oil poured over his head was a bit messy. The years erased all visages of the oil, but the shadow of that experience brought more turmoil than it brought dream fulfillment. David had to choose faith over immediate goal achievement.

As men and women of faith, we deliberately spend our lives on the Teacher's mission. Some must leave their boats and businesses behind as did Peter and his friends. Others dedicate their lives to the Spirit's leading such that they become people "of honest report, full of the Holy Ghost and wisdom," the kind that can be appointed over significant mission endeavors (Acts 6:3). All people of faith develop ears that can hear the Spirit's leading and eyes that can see the world's constant need for living witnesses.

When these two things come together, listening to the Spirit's leading and seeing the world's needs, something miraculous happens. Dreams come to life. Hope rises. Purpose solidifies. These miracles connect with the Spirit's gifting in a person's life. Hope-filled dreamers begin to pursue those points of newfound passion and purpose. Sometimes this process takes years of apprenticeship and faithful study of the Word. Such apprenticeships transform us as men and women of faith. We become the dream. Living the dream repeatedly calls us to spiritual formation that resists other dreams and passions. This living calls for a walk of humble service. The path also calls for equipping others to continue the dream.

Sometimes dreams crash.

At first I was going to write "sometimes dreams fade," but crashing or shattering better names the reality. Sometimes dreams crash because others fail. Paul feared all his labor produced nothing but air. He wondered if he would have to give birth to the Galatian church again. (See Galatians 4:11, 19.) All that painful labor and dreams of a church seemed ready to crash.

Sometimes dreams crash because of our misunderstanding of God's mission and care for the world. How many of us have suffered unending pain when a child, spouse, or spiritual leader turned back on faith after walking so faithfully for years? Shards of broken dreams cut into our feet with each step we take. Attempts to wear thicker-soled shoes only reinforce how those fragments can pierce though our defenses when we least expect it. Our deals with God lay shredded on the grieving ground;

we believed He would protect us from those kinds of losses if we pursued the dream with everything we had.

Sometimes dreams crash when life robs us of open ministry doors. Some have prepared for mission fields closed by foreign governments or by church board decisions. We all know people who have selflessly equipped themselves for service and then illness in their family limits the field of vision to just "caring for one of the little ones" rather than living the worship dream. Sacrifice takes on a whole new dimension.

This spiritual formation in times of suffering calls us to choose faith. We rejoice with those who live the dream, then raise our head toward heaven to find one sliver of God's face that shines on us. We must choose faith when God does not answer prayers as we hoped. He does not make a wayward loved one come back to faith. He does not make all governments or church boards change their policies. He does not heal all our children. Instead He hears our cry; then He calls us to choose faith.

In 1989 my young family and I left our former lives behind and followed the dream. God placed the dream of military chaplaincy deep in my soul. The dream would not be quiet. We moved. We gave up the house, pastoral ministry, a tenured public-school teaching position, and familiar surroundings to live in two college dorm rooms. My precious wife and four young children adapted to a new way of life so I could complete a second graduate degree. We did so because our ears heard God's voice and our eyes saw places of suffering that needed the Prince of Peace. My acceptance to seminary and induction into the US Army Reserves Chaplain Candidacy program confirmed the dream. Full-time Bible college teaching and full-time seminary studying were small prices to pay. Who needs more than two rooms when the dream calls you?

Then the dream crashed harder than a child's Humpty Dumpty rhyme. One moment I was living the dream and the next I was lying on the ground with shattered elbows. Though I stayed in the army reserves another four years, the nondeployable classification detonated all my efforts to hold the dream together. I cannot describe the pain; months of physical therapy at the Dover Air Force Base hospital did not fit on the same scale as the pain in my spirit, emotions, and will.

God would not put my dream back together again.

I did not want to live.

All I could do was choose to take one more step in faith, even though the broken dream embedded itself in every part of my body. In my perspective I was useless. I could work two jobs, care for a family, and do without "normal" things, but I could not live without a dream.

The Teacher wanted me to live. But He would not sweep the dream fragments from my path. He would only hold me while I sobbed until all strength was gone.

The Teacher held me through eighteen years of sobbing. He held me through that seminary degree program. He would not let me quit because someday new dreams would come, and dreamers do not quit. He held me through a ministry relocation. He held me through a PhD program. He held me through working with a team of other dreamers to found an accredited Apostolic seminary. Some friends tried to console me because I now had the privilege of teaching military chaplains who could carry the dream. I sobbed yet again; the broken dream made it difficult for me to celebrate people who carried similar dreams.

Then one day the Teacher said my sobbing days were over. After eighteen years I could breathe again. Choosing to walk by faith took me past the place where dream shards could no longer cut me. I do not know why the Teacher did not heal me physically so I could finally live out the dream He had given me. I do not know why the Teacher let the pain continue for so long. I do not know why a new dream could not rise from the ashes. All I know is the Teacher told me to keep walking even when I felt worthless without the dream. The Teacher called me to hear His valuation of my life without the dream before I could dream again.

Fortunately, most people recover from shattered dreams more quickly than I did. Inexplicably some suffer for the remainder of their days. The Teacher, however, calls us to choose faith. Faith that has no evidence. Faith that has no feeling. Faith that does not illuminate more than the next step.

Maybe this kind of faith choice can be seen in the life of Israel. The newly liberated people of God get a mention in the faith hall of fame: "By faith they passed through the Red sea as by dry land: which the Egyptians assaying to do were drowned" (Hebrews 11:29). Spiritual formation in suffering requires one more step. A study of Exodus shows the children of Israel had no other option. Mountains bracketed them on either side. Egypt's elite fighting forces looked forward to practicing their slaughter techniques on the Israelites. The distant shore might as well have been on the moon. With terror they took a step into the dry seabed. Then they took another step.

The author of Hebrews, looking back on that fateful day, called the steps faith rather than terror. Steps that start in terror, if aimed in God's direction, become steps of faith over time.

Choose a terrorized step of faith if you must. The Teacher walks with you as shattered dreams lose their power and ankles learn the feeling of faith yet again.

Personal Reflection

Examine your current life and ministry.

    a. *How does your current situation match up to dreams you have had in the past?*

    b. *As challenging as it may be, list faith choices right in front of you.*

    c. *Pray for guidance for your next step of faith. What does that step look like?*

    d. *If wounds from past broken dreams still hinder your progress, how can you share those challenges with another person of faith? How can you pray about these painful experiences yet again?*

DO NOT WASTE YOUR SUFFERING

Our world suffers from garbage overload. Trash from past dreams and unwanted byproducts of current efforts create crises in many countries. One rebellion against this trashy view of life can be seen in the contemporary trend called upcycling. Many people celebrate the transformation of discarded wooden pallets into furniture and hardwood flooring. Perhaps the most inspiring example is Landfill Harmonic, a youth orchestra from Cateura, Paraguay.

The orchestra children share Paraguay's capital city dump with 2,500 families. Each day the dump receives 1,500 tons of garbage. The dump provides their food and their housing materials. Children work with their parents to salvage refuse that they can sell to meet their daily needs. Living on the city's trash produces a cloud of despair along with contaminated drinking water. The young musicians' lives changed with the discovery of a broken violin and the vision of a music teacher. Trash heap artists began turning random scraps of steel, kitchen utensils, and broken pieces of wood into musical instruments. They not only reclaim materials discarded by the city, they also ensure their children do not become throwaways.

Paul feared the Galatian church had suffered many things in vain by abandoning their life in the Spirit in favor of their own efforts. Sometimes crashed dreams and God's adamant preference for sufficient grace in our suffering cause saints to work harder and harder to make up for the lack of dream fulfillment. Such efforts waste our suffering. Hopes and decisions focused away from simple faith steps squander opportunities to experience spiritual formation. Such choices naturally flow from our inability to understand God's purposes in times of loss and suffering.

Christ's greatest works of the Cross and Resurrection provided the context for His disciples' dream crash. They went from tremendous faith to abject doubt. In effect, all but one betrayed Jesus. The Teacher stepped into their protected space. Often we say they locked the door to protect them from the soldiers that killed Jesus. Maybe they locked the door against crashed dreams. Soldiers did not need to kill them—their disappointment was doing a better job than another trio of crosses could ever do. The Teacher invited Thomas to put his fingers into His recently acquired wounds as a sign that he should move forward in faith. Of course, the disciples still misunderstood some of the next steps, but they would learn not to waste their suffering. (See Acts 1:6, for example.) In fact, they would learn to count it all joy.

Personal Reflection

Consider a biblical character that suffered as he or she followed God's call. How did that suffering provide surprising strength for the journey that lay ahead?

CONCLUSION

Some followed Jesus expecting a wonderful and exciting journey. After all, who would not like hanging out with the Teacher who multiplied bread, walked on water, made blind people see, and rebuked self-righteous people? Just imagine what the Messiah would do when He got ready to take care of all the evil people in places of power!

One such potential disciple encountered a surprising response when he came to Jesus. "A certain man said unto him, Lord, I will follow thee whithersoever thou goest. And Jesus said unto him, Foxes have holes, and birds of the air have nests; but the Son of man hath not where to lay his head" (Luke 9:57–58). Rather than passing into a charmed life with a Pied Piper–like figure, he turned away from one who would not promise an easy way. Jesus would not be his kind of savior.

Spiritual formation calls us to tip over all idols. Times of suffering and crashed dreams will be a gift for those who choose the way of faith. In crushing times, saints have the opportunity to give up childhood myths about God. Sometimes we say we should "just let God be God." Of course God will be God whether we give permission or not. The school of suffering strips away all comfort blankets. We stand empty before the Teacher. We learn what it is like to follow the pillowless One. We worship when we do not understand what He is doing. We grow from childlike faith to more mature faith. The Teacher loves us so much that He will not rescue us from the pain that comes with walking into new places.

Suffering brings us to the crossroads where we must choose to trust the Teacher's ordering of our steps. We will go into a deeper relationship with Him, or we will turn back to keep our place of comfort where we think we know God because of the good things He does for us. Perhaps those who turn away from suffering's growth potential will be saved. They will still have moments of difficulty in life, but they will never really know Jesus, the One who suffers with them. James, the brother of Jesus, offered this wonderful transition for those who choose faith in suffering: "My brethren, count it all joy when ye fall into divers temptations; knowing this, that the trying of your faith worketh patience. But let patience have her perfect work, that ye may be perfect and entire, wanting nothing" (James 1:3–4).

Personal Reflection

1. *Reread your initial definition of suffering at the beginning of this chapter.*

   a. *How has your understanding changed during your reading, reflection, and prayer in this chapter?*

2. *What spiritual formation steps will you take in light of your revised understanding? Consider sharing your findings with a spiritual friend.*

PRAYER

I pray the Lord gives you strength to love Him even when He calls you to walk in places where pillows cannot be found. I pray you let Him hold your hand while He takes you through difficult situations. I pray you know to ask for wisdom in those times (James 1:5). I pray you trust the Teacher when He points out areas where your faith needs to grow out of the nursery. I pray that shattered dreams, though they may pierce your soul, open the way to a new relationship with the Teacher. I pray you always choose to respond favorably to the Teacher's invitation rather than seeking protection from the pain.

Amen

13 | *Talking and Writing*

I must confess I love all things related to paper and pens. This Christmas I received four boxes of stationery and a new wax seal from my loving wife. Birthdays and other special occasions bring a new fountain pen or ink. Rummaging through antique stores includes the occasional joy of finding vintage blank journal pages that can be repurposed in a new format or a pre–World War II pen that begs to live again.

Fortunately, I live in a time when common people can afford paper and can write. Even expensive stationery that may cost one dollar or more per page can be experienced by most people if they wanted to do so. The ancient world presented a far different scenario—even for the 10 percent of the population that could read and write. Some estimates place the cost of one sheet of papyrus at roughly one day's wages! To put this in perspective, when the apostles wrote the New Testament, ten sheets of good papyrus would cost about as much as a five-hundred-dollar cell phone for the working-class laborer today. Why, we can even pack dishes in big sheets of the stuff.

Yet Paul boldly stated saints could be epistles "known and read of all men" (II Corinthians 3:2). Rather than carrying ink stains or chisel indentations, they carried the Spirit's marks on the heart. Our whole lives become a means of communicating the gospel of Christ. In this chapter we will explore spiritual formation in ways we communicate with others through our lifestyle, spoken conversations, written word, and participation in virtual or digital space. As we become more like the Teacher, our communication with others conveys Christ through us. This communication produces the possibility to be agents of reconciliation in our world.

Personal Reflection

1. *Reflect over the last few years. How does your "living epistle" present God's gracious care to the world?*

2. *How does your life demonstrate the wonder of becoming more like Christ?*

OUR LIFESTYLE COMMUNICATES

I have to smile when I see ways our world "discovers" truths the Bible has contained for so long. For example, neuroscience now helps teachers and counselors understand ways to help their clients break out of destructive thought patterns. By introducing new ways to think about circumstances, people can actually remap their minds. Over time, mind remapping will produce new ways of thinking about the world around them. Paul must have understood the same principle when he admonished his readers to think on honest, just, pure, lovely, virtuous, and praiseworthy things. As they learned these new thought patterns, God would be with them (Philippians 4:8–9).

Spiritual formation not only transforms us but also influences the world around us. Previous chapters explored ways to renew our minds by thinking about, listening to, and being aware of Christ at all times. In this chapter we explore the impact our transformation should have on the world around us.

From the time God called Abram out of Ur, the Creator has chosen His people to be a contrast people—a people markedly different from the world. They could not live for themselves or use spiritual gifts for their own benefit if they were to witness the beauty of following their Holy God.

Being Christ's disciple requires surrendering personal preferences. Old preferences of conversation and lifestyle centered around "lusts of the flesh, fulfilling the desires of the flesh and of the mind; and were by nature the children of wrath, even as others" (Ephesians 2:3). Spiritual formation reminds us that many of these preferences must die along with our old nature. We have an opportunity beyond surrendering our personal preferences. God has raised us up in Christ and causes us to sit together in heavenly places (Ephesians 2:5–6).

Being reinvigorated to life does not tell the whole story. Spiritual formation moves beyond the "fix" to live on display as God's handiwork. The Artist refashions us to good works (Ephesians 2:10). In other words, we do not concentrate on surrendering our preferences as much as we anticipate and work toward living out God's preferences. What a joyful transition!

Spiritual formation forces a deep change in us. We may have started this walk to be saved from the old habits of sin and be acceptable to Christ on the Last Day, but we cannot stay in that frame of mind. If our goal is to avoid sin, then we will not mature in Christ. Instead we take up new preferences and practices together. Old things have passed away, but we must learn new preferences. This is what it means to be formed in Christ.

By the mid-twentieth century, various forms of electronic media began to bring about unforeseen changes in society. In 1964 Marshall McLuhan, an English professor at the University of Toronto, coined the phrase, "the medium is the message" to help describe what was taking place. McLuhan understood the *message* to be changes that take place in society. As society was changing, McLuhan believed observers should be able to see the new messages at work to bring about those changes. He considered *medium* to be the extensions of ourselves rather than just the content heard or seen in the medium.

Christ was the true exemplar of "the medium is the message" phenomenon. He came into the world to bring about universal change. He did not just speak words of love; He was love. Demons, religious rulers, blind beggars, and expectant crowds all had to respond to His presence.

And He sends us to do greater works than He did (John 14:12).

A disciple's lifestyle becomes the "epistle known and read of all men," a part of Christ's medium to change the world. As disciples seek to love God and neighbor, they become more and more like Christ. They experience spiritual formation that encompasses everything they are and do. They hold nothing back as private prerogatives or personal rights. They know the message changed them, so they purposefully look forward to new opportunities to be God's medium in the world. They joyfully anticipate being that kind of medium.

Personal Reflection

From time to time we need to celebrate our growth in Christ. One way to do this is to see old personal preferences that we release as we follow Christ's preferences. Identify one such preference change.

   a. *How did this change come to pass?*
   b. *How did God use other believers to assist you in identifying the preference and making the change?*
   c. *Finally, what are some lasting implications of this change in your life?*

THE POWER OF THE TONGUE

Archimedes believed he could move the whole world if he had a long enough lever, a fulcrum, and a place to stand. Perhaps the starting place is a little closer to home. James 3 carefully examines the power of the human tongue. Such a little member of our bodies can ignite forest fires or bring great healing. James still calls us to recognize the failure in using the same mouth to glorify God and to place curses on others (James 3:9–10). Spiritual formation removes the earthy, old-natured conversations that expose bitterness, envy, and strife—the sources of confusion and all evil work.

A casual reading of James 3 leaves us with little hope that the tongue's power can be used for good. The apostle comes pretty close to the Teacher's hyperbolic call for cutting off arms and putting out eyes that offend when he posits, "The tongue can no man tame; it is an unruly evil, full of deadly poison" (3:8). People can tame beasts and even serpents, but they cannot tame the tongue.

Fortunately, spiritual formation draws on resources from outside of the individual.

Spiritual formation always draws from the power of the Spirit rather than personal efforts. We rely on God's grace to transform us. James calls for wisdom "from above" (3:17) to produce good fruits from the tongue just as he did to transform "divers temptations" into discipleship maturity. (See James 1:2–5.) James proposes a far better use of the tongue than the bitter, envious, angry, deceitful, sensual, and devilish bilge that spews out of the corrupt heart. As James tells us, this kind of wisdom comes from below. Spiritual formation of the tongue requires honesty, commitment to let the Spirit complete the work, and new behaviors. Such change also requires wisdom from above.

Assessment provides a starting point for harnessing the tongue's power for good rather than a destructive forest fire. Begin by listening to the Spirit's assessment of every word you say: words at home, words at work, words with friends, words in the marketplace, and even words while driving down the road with no one else in the car. Let the Spirit underscore places where words curse rather than bless, where words convey envy, bitterness, discord, self-centeredness, self-justification, and partial truth. Listening to the Spirit will reveal that bad language far exceeds a limited list of curse words. Confess the brokenness of your language. Make a record of the ways the enemy of your soul uses your unruly member to do his evil work. Repent. Ask forgiveness of the Teacher as well as those your tongue has scorched.

The tongue's power comes from a deeper place than the mouth. In Matthew 12 Jesus identified the critical Pharisees as evil people because their mouths spoke from their hearts. Disciples will take the second step to examine their hearts as they seek to expose the source of harmful language. Sadly, many people in our culture justify harmful language under a misguided rubric of honesty. We may have heard people explain they simply speak the truth of what they feel. While they may have correctly concluded everyone will know what they think, they incorrectly assumed honesty justifies words vomited from a corrupt heart.

Perhaps a review of Jesus' Kingdom teaching can help underscore the central need of this spiritual formation effort. Jesus extended the sayings of old to address the deeper issue at work. I often hear people affirm Jesus' assertion that adultery happens in the heart prior to any physical act. We can rightly conclude people should not think about adulterous acts any more than they should actually do it. A system of accountability (software, partners, or a combination thereof) helps men and women keep themselves pure from sexual immorality.

We do not give murder the same level of attention. Anger in the heart can lead to calling someone worthless or a fool. (See Matthew 5:21–24.) To even casually consider a person as worthless places us in danger of judgment or Hell's fires. Lord, forgive us!

We will need the Spirit to expose such levels of heart corruption. The Teacher loves us so much that He does not want us to harbor anger or thoughts of anyone being worthless. Listen to the Spirit as God exposes the heart's corruption behind habits of the tongue.

The third step in harnessing the power of the tongue for good is to change both the heart and the tongue. Perhaps James's admonition to confess our faults to one another can help bring such corrections. Confessing the Spirit's revelation of our tongue and heart provides the place for others to care for us in prayer and provoke to good works. As a teenager I heard that a cousin of mine wrestled with the tendency to exaggerate. To break the habit, she began to confess the exaggeration was a lie and that the truth was not in her. She found the need to exaggerate dissipated as she confessed the tongue and heart problem to those around her.

This critical spiritual formation step reorients us from pursuing our own right standing before God, something done by Christ's work on the cross, to living as Kingdom agents in the world. Our lives become the medium to bring about change in the world. James 3 concludes by extolling the impact of a transformed heart. Where the tongue once brought "confusion and every evil work," the tongue now has the capacity to participate in "the fruit of righteousness [that] is sown in peace of them that make peace" (3:15–18). These conversations that lead to peace naturally flow from hearts shaped by new wisdom from above. Instead of reacting to the brokenness around them, disciples react to the pure, peaceable, gentle, easily entreated, merciful, good-fruited, prejudice-free, and sincere reality that has been formed in them.

Jesus pronounced blessings on peacemakers—people who live on behalf of others in hours of need. Fellowship in the body provides the proving ground for such peacemaking efforts. Both Jesus and James spoke of challenges the early church faced while living peaceably with each other.

Evidently human nature has not changed that much over the millennia. Jesus took a position that would be considered dangerous by many leaders today. He believed reconciliation, when considering someone as worthless or a fool, should take precedence over offerings. Presenting a worshipful offering would be mockery from those who devalued a brother or sister. (See Matthew 5:22–24.) Reconciliation to others will always be at the core of transforming the tongue and the heart. Practicing reconciliation prior to worship prepares the church for witnessing grace in the world.

Personal Reflection

Make an outline of the three tongue-taming steps identified in this section. Apply the steps to an area of your conversation that needs to be brought into closer relationship with Christ.

DIGITAL SPACE

Until the beginning of the twentieth century, virtues and character were accorded greater importance than self-fulfillment. People found spouses based on character measures rather than affections or a quest for a soulmate. In fact, women's diaries frequently conveyed the need to select a steady and dependable person over someone that turned heads when he walked into the room. With the development of psychology and a sense of an individual self, personality became more significant than virtues. Today people go on journeys to "find themselves." They are burdened to be true to themselves in ways their grandparents never even considered. Many people have taken personality tests; few have taken virtue tests.

Western culture continues its shift in personal identity away from one's family and social group, where virtues matter, to a place where people project a personally constructed self-identity in the virtual world. The trajectory from character to personality in the digital age has produced a new kind of persona called an avatar. According to Techopedia, an "avatar is a personalized graphical illustration that represents a computer user, or a character or alter ego that represents that user." In the digital world people create an identity for specific contexts. Those identities—avatars—may differ depending on the occasion. While some people more carefully consider what they do in all of their virtual worlds, blogs, and chatrooms for fear of a future employer investigating their various identities and interactions, many still do not present a unified self. For followers of Christ, the only self they have is that of a disciple. All other "selves" had to die in the baptismal tank.

While the early church did not have to deal with virtual reality, they did have to examine how disciples presented themselves to the wider world. For example, to follow Christ meant a convert had to give up participation in any of the mystery religions of the day. They also had to refrain from the Caesar cult and the legal demand to burn incense to the governmental head. This decision cost some disciples their lives. Such disciples willingly gave up their civil rights in exchange for their new identity as a people redeemed by Christ and to be a part of His church.

The apostles addressed the need to live out Jesus' character in their surrounding culture. For example, Peter assumed disciples would be treated as evildoers. Rather than reacting to such slander, he called his readers to maintain honest conversation among the Gentiles with the possible outcome that others would see their good works and glorify God (I Peter 2:12). Peter warned against disciples losing their identity by being caught up in the conversations of their neighbors. The apostle cited Lot's example where a good man "vexed his righteous soul from day to day with their evil deeds" (II Peter 2:7–8). When disciples created avatar-like participation in evil worlds populated by "brute beasts" that riot in the daytime, fill their eyes with adultery, cease not from sin, beguiling stable souls, exercise covetousness, and curse children (II Peter 2:12–14), they would suffer loss as did Lot and Balaam.

Discipleship formation in digital space requires taking both of these realities into consideration. Followers of Christ in the twenty-first century must perfect righteousness in digital spaces as well as face-to-face conversations. Living as sons and daughters of God "in the midst of a crooked and perverse nation" provides the opportunity to "shine as lights in the world" like never before (Philippians 2:15). Not pursuing spiritual formation in digital space will likely result in default surrender to those forces of darkness.

One way to consider the influence of social media is through social impact theory. In his theory, Bibb Latané suggests that three factors play a role in determining the power of influence: strength (or importance of the group speaking), immediacy, and number of people doing the influencing. Social media provides the opportunity to maximize all three factors for good or for evil. Spiritual formation in digital space calls for attention to all three areas.

Spiritual formation forces disciples to uncover the sources of strength in their social space. This excavation process helps the disciple become a spiritual producer rather than a default consumer of corrupting spiritualities of a broken world. One can ask a series of questions after engaging in a form of social media. First, does the experience leave you spiritually stronger or weaker? This question takes you beyond the more basic and juvenile question of which sites to visit or could Jesus visit the site with you. Spiritual strength can indicate the opportunity to be influenced by the right people as well as making a positive influence. Second, does participation in the site provide an opportunity to disciple other people? This discipleship work exists on a long continuum from pre-converts (even very secular people) to mature saints. In other words, does participation in the site provide a place for others to see God's grace in your life? Even engagement in a Christian website needs to be evaluated in this way. If you can bring healing, hope, and purpose to others, then this could be a valuable place for ministry. On the other hand, if divisions, bitterness, and pride develop out of the participation, then the Master will not be glorified.

Latané's second factor, immediacy, relates to the stewardship of time. Social media provides the opportunity for impact because of the potential to immediately respond to posts made by others. Being available to immediately respond requires one to assess how much time should be available to social media and how that time is allocated. Responding quickly to needs on Facebook, for example, can place one's voice and spiritual gifts in the position to care for others. Over time these conversations can build caring opportunities. Yet, disciples cannot be available at all times or other aspects of life will not receive the attention they need. Social media use will require an audit of both the amount and quality of time we make ourselves available to others in this venue. Peer accountability can help the disciple remain honest in this audit. Do we use social media to escape from the reality of daily life, or are we truly being available to disciple others?

Number represents the final factor in Latané's theory. In face-to-face communication we rarely listen to more than a handful of people on a given topic. A greater number of sources may increase the impact of those interactions—to a point. When one more voice gets added to the voices of hundreds, the influence has reached a point of diminishing returns. Clicking "like" on a person's post with two hundred other people will add little value. On the other hand, prayerfully submitting "a word fitly spoken" (Proverbs 25:11) can bring healing and hope to someone in need. Those words can also open the space for further communication with those in need.

As part of the contemporary world, many disciples will have some digital footprint. Spiritual formation calls us to have those steps ordered of the Lord as with all other steps we take. If participation brings glory to God, then the disciple should courageously participate with words that witness to God's goodness. If participation either generates animosity or gets lost in a flood of words, then the disciple should probably dedicate her worthy service to God in other venues. Spend time judiciously in social media that builds you as a follower of Christ or provides space to help others see the gospel light. Disciples will avoid many websites that damage God's gifts. They will avoid or limit participation in social media that provides little impact on others. Finally, they will set a watch on their media consumption and participation to keep from squandering time that needs to be available for others in need.

Personal Reflection

1. *How does a discipleship approach to social media differ from a legalistic approach with externally mandated rules?*

2. *Evaluate your social media usage from the last week.*
   a. *How would you describe your growth as a disciple from your postings?*
   b. *What can you celebrate?*
   c. *How could you have followed Christ more faithfully?*

3. *How might the discipleship approach guide your social media use in the coming weeks?*

4. *If you do not use any social media, consider the differences between legalism and discipleship approaches to the use of written media, broadcast media, or music.*

WRITTEN WORD

Before leaving a few concluding comments at the end of the chapter, I would like to open the door to spiritual formation in a lost art form: letter writing. I realize that few disciples write letters in a world where instant communication and ubiquitous cell phone usage has won the day. A text to a friend can certainly address Latané's call for immediacy in understanding the power to influence a target audience. Disciples should participate in the twenty-first century's gifts of instant communication in a judicious way; however, they can also benefit from recalling the first century's gift of writing.

First-century correspondence would have carried considerable weight given the cost of paper and getting the letter to recipients. While governmental correspondence had access to sophisticated delivery methods on Rome's expanding road systems, private letters needed to be carried by merchant friends who happened to be going that way or sent via a servant with the letter. By comparison, a two-cent sheet of paper and a fifty-cent stamp is inexpensive indeed!

I have chosen to write letters as both a spiritual discipline and as an effort to retain some portions of civility from past generations. I am frequently surprised by how often people hang on to letters I have sent them. Some have found their ways to refrigerator doors, bedside tables, and Bible covers. I have written letters to my family, preachers who have spoken a powerful word into my life, children who sing in church, colleagues at school or church, and dear friends. During an anxious sabbatical period, the Lord called me to write a letter every day for nearly two months to express thanksgiving for a different person's influence in my life, to examine methods God used them to care for others in ways that frequently went unnoticed, and to pray a blessing into their lives.

My letter writing experienced a significant transformation after the study of Paul's letters. While reading D. A. Carson's *Praying with Paul: A Call to Spiritual Reformation* for one of my seminary classes, I began to see the power conveyed in the close relationship between the author and his first readers (or hearers, assuming the letters were first orally performed for their audience). Most of Paul's letters included prayers of thanksgiving for the recipients as well as prayers for God's continued blessings. Usually these two prayers directly correlated with each other. Paul recognized God's work in the readers' lives, gave thanks, and then prayed God would continue to do that work in them.

Write a letter.

My letter writing became a type of spiritual formation when I followed Paul's use of pen and paper. Every recipient has benefited from the work of the Spirit in his or her life in some way. Usually they have shared that gift with me as well. Finally, I pray the Spirit continues to bless them in Kingdom-shaped ways. Such missives of blessings changed lives in Paul's day, and they can change lives today.

Try writing a letter each week. Prayerfully consider the recipient's contributions to the Kingdom and ways that contribution has gifted you. Attending to God's work in and through others transforms the writer as well as the recipient. Conclude the letter with a prayer of blessing. Follow the Spirit's leading rather than the exact same formula for each letter. Humbly seal the envelope in a spirit of intercession. Release the letter into the mailbox as an act of faith. You will find yourself being changed through Spirit-led letter writing. You will witness the Spirit's power when such letters speak to friends in times of need.

By the way, do not be afraid to practice your penmanship in the process.

CONCLUSION

God made humanity in His image. One of the first things we read about the Creator is His ability to speak transformation into the chaotic world around Him. Disciples who follow the Creator will need to spend seasons of their lives considering the ways they use the gift of speech. This spiritual formation process helps disciples live out the calling to be spiritual producers, to be epistles written and read of all men and women.

One study found both women and men speak about sixteen thousand words per day.[1] At that rate the average person speaks enough to fill a two-hundred-page book every three or four days! Spiritual formation calls us to consider the way we live out God's purposes with this most basic of gifts. As with all gifts from God, the gift of speech can bring blessings if used appropriately; sadly, it can bring much harm as well.

PRAYER

Let us pray,

Lord, You spoke and powerful things happened. We set a watch on all of our communication so that we participate in Your kingdom work. Protect our minds and hearts from all the angry and proudful words around us. Purify our inner beings again so that we can speak out of an abundant, joy-filled existence. Let all our words bring healing and hope to those around us. We desire to learn the pleasure of being "letters written and read" of all people. Thank you for all the ways we can speak in our day—we can use modern technology as well as "old school" tools to bring grace to our hearers.

In Jesus' name,

Amen

14 | *Remembering and Storytelling*

All spiritual formation revolves around one thing—relationship. Walking with Christ ensures a right relationship with Him. A right relationship with Him places the student in right relationship with His other disciples. Unified disciples will continue the work of their Master just as the apostles did in the transition from Jesus' work in Luke to the Spirit's work through the church in Acts.

Have you ever had moments where you feel like you have already experienced what is happening right in front of you? So many people have had the phenomenon that we have a term for it: déjà vu. Some scientists believe the experience comes from the brain trying to move short-term memory into long-term memory; for a moment the memory is in both the past and the present. While I really do not understand what happens in déjà vu experiences, I do believe disciples will feel a spiritual longing or prompting in the direction of God's purposes. Spiritual formation teaches us to hear the Spirit even as we walk in the Spirit.

We will conclude this discussion of spiritual formation by examining the gift of being a people of memory while we walk boldly, yet humbly, toward God's purpose at the end of time. By completing the book in this way, we look forward to the Spirit's work to continually transform us as men and women of faith. This final examination takes us through three biblical threads: remembering, living as a storied people, and the value of reflecting on our lives as Jesus' followers. A look at writing a spiritual autobiography will be the last formation strategy of the book.

Personal Reflection

1. *Think back to (1) your conversion, (2) a challenging time, and (3) a time when you felt your ministry or spiritual walk indicated faithful stewardship.*

    a. *How was God at work in each of these three events?*

    b. *How did these events contribute to making you the person of faith you are today?*

    c. *What are some elements from these times that you would not include as part of your current identity? (For example, Israel might not have included Egypt's melons and onions in their identity.)*

2. *Now remember a key element of your congregation's history that represents a trial and another that represents a victory.*

    a. *Where was God at work in the two stories?*

    b. *How does your congregation use the stories to contribute to its identity as a body of believers?*

THE CALL TO REMEMBER

Even a simple search for "remember" in the Bible will illustrate the importance of remembering in every part of Scripture. God promised to remember His covenant with Noah (Genesis 9:15), and Jesus called for saints in Ephesus and Sardis to remember and return to their former relationship with Him. Spiritual formation includes the importance of remembering the right things. According to Allen Verhey, biblical remembrance goes far beyond recollection of past events. Remembrance as God's people forms a collective identity and determines future conduct.

Failure to remember could be considered a form of community dementia. Not remembering prevents the community and its members from continuing to be formed as God's people. Consequently, they will no longer have conduct that follows Jesus' example. They have wandered away from their Teacher.

Worship serves as a memory aid. Songs, prayers, testimonies, fellowship, sermons, and celebration of the Lord's Supper continually form worshipers in right relationship with the One who called them. Rather than remembering the wrong things, disciples have the Spirit to assist them in bringing all the right things to their remembrance (John 14:26). For example, Israel thought their souls were dried away; they had inappropriate memories of their lives in Egypt and failed to remember the Lord who freed them (Numbers 11:6). Not remembering the Lord's work is equated with apostasy and failure to fulfill covenant commitments.

Remembering keeps disciples focused on living into the future God has planned for the world. Rather than a personal exercise in life review, remembering carefully examines God's work in our lives and our response to that work.

WONDER-FILLED STORIES

Paul used the olive tree as an object lesson as he explained the relationship between Israel, God's covenant people, and new Gentile converts. (See Romans 11:16–24.) God used the unnatural process of grafting a new branch into an old root. Normal olive tree husbandry used the strength of a new root system to support the engrafted cultivated branches. God did a strange work in bringing the wild branches into the ancient root. Gentile believers gained access to thousands of years of faith. They became a new people by God's gracious work.

The author of Hebrews retold the story from faithful Abel up to contemporary members of a "great cloud of witnesses." Living among this storied people helped new saints lay aside weights and sins. God's storied people accept Jesus as the One who re-authors their story. (See Romans 11:4–12:2.)

When disciples accept the Author's offer to join the story, they experience the wonder of being re-membered. Wimberly uses this image to graphically convey the gospel's regenerating power. God puts His people back into His body where they belong. They no longer need to feel dis-membered or alone. They now have a story to constitute their lives and to guide future actions. Spiritual formation intentionally follows this process to make sure Jesus serves as the author and finisher of the new story.

In the Old Testament we read of Israel's commitment to retelling stories in times of crises as well as change. Festivals and sacrifices retold the story of being brought from

Egypt and becoming a new people with purpose. The story included points where Israel failed to follow the narrative designed by their covenant Lord. According to the covenant conditions, they could expect to be cut off from being God's people when they failed to be faithful in their identity and actions. Yet God worked to re-member His people through His sovereign reclamation project. The end of the process proved God's ability to re-member the people and dis-member (cut away) their sins. (See Jeremiah 31:20–34.) Rewriting their story included writing out the power of sin!

As the Israelites returned from Babylon, they often retold the stories in prayer and in conversations with each other. Nehemiah reminded God of the covenant as he travailed for Jerusalem (Nehemiah 1:8–9). Later, when his work drew to a close, he appointed leaders to various tasks and prayed for God's memory. Nehemiah asked for God to remember and honor his years of labor (Nehemiah 13:14). Joining in memory work with God gave him the courage and directions he still needed to take. Though the walls and gates stood strong, Sabbath practices lay in ruin; they could not exist without knowing and living the Sabbath. Israel's story set them apart. When the Israelites lost their story, they began to intermarry with neighboring idol worshipers and spiritual leaders lost their focus. Nehemiah acted in line with the story. Then he prayed one more time for God to remember his contributions (Nehemiah 13:31).

The early church also lived the story to participate in Christ's mission. Paul shared stories to help them remember how Jesus had created them as a new people destined to do good works. Paul knew they once were a dis-membered people, they were without Christ. He helped them revise their story as they became part of the covenant of promise. Paul's stories exemplify Verhey's memory outcomes: in Ephesians 2 the church renewed its identity and demonstrated conduct in line with this story.

Stories bring comfort when God's people face disappointments and uncertainty. Psalms of lament (for example, Psalm 42) include a process of examining current brokenness, remembering past blessings, confessing current feelings of forgottenness, and an anticipated time of praise. Through observation and experience, the psalmist learned that trusting in chariots and horses led to disappointing outcomes in the story; instead he would "remember the name of the LORD" (Psalm 20:7).

Spiritual formation, as outlined in this book, assists disciples in the process of hearing the divine story and surrendering to the new narrative God has for their lives. Reading the Bible, prayer, repenting, forgiving, working, resting, etc., all contribute to living in the Spirit as a new creation.

Personal Reflection

Think about choices you need to make in your family, work, and ministry in the next six months.

    a. *How do your memories provide resources for you to determine future decisions and behavior?*

    b. *Pray over your answer and seek the Spirit's direction as you make critical decisions.*

    c. *Consider sharing your responses and prayer requests with a spiritual friend.*

THE GIFT OF REFLECTION

Perhaps the Lord's Supper provides the most powerful biblical example of participating in God's redemptive story. Jesus called the apostles to practice the Supper "in remembrance of me" (Luke 22:19). Remembering Jesus' blood sacrifice and broken body renewed the worshipers' identity and called for new conduct in line with the work of their Master.

The Lord is present when we celebrate the Supper. The early church practiced this on a regular basis as part of their new identity along with the apostles' doctrine, fellowship, and prayer (Acts 2:42). The practice continued throughout the places where Paul ministered (Acts 20:7). Paul believed sharing the cup and bread placed worshipers in fellowship or communion with Christ as well as each other (I Corinthians 10:16–17). We receive the gift of reflection as one dimension of God's grace when we celebrate the Supper together. In the Supper the Spirit calls us to examine our lives in light of God's redemptive work, identify areas where the Spirit calls us to maturity, and take intentional steps toward being more like our Teacher.

Luke 10 gives another example of Jesus' use of reflective practice with His first class of students. He sent out the seventy with clear instructions. They engaged in ministry as directed. They returned to tell the story of their experiences. Finally, Jesus modified their awareness as needed.

Sometimes the corrective actions call for deeper levels of change. Earlier in this book we explored Jesus' reflective practice with the disciples after they failed to cast out a demon. (See chapter 6; see also Mark 9:28–29.) The disciples had failed in faithful response to Jesus' teaching and prayer. Reflective practice identified the problem and proposed next steps.

As noted in the preface, this book may require various seasons of implementation of spiritual formation to have substantial lasting value. Now that you have completed the book, consider the following questions:

1. Which spiritual formation practice does the Spirit call to your attention at this time?

2. How do the Word and Spirit identify areas of potential growth? Reflecting on specific events or stories from the past can help spiritual formation move out of theory into practice at this point.

3. What next steps can you take to become more like Christ? You may want to follow suggested steps from sections in this book or develop action items on your own.

4. How can you use other saints to help you be accountable to the spiritual formation initiative? Consider sharing your examination of the Word and Spirit, your past and present spiritual state, and action items. Set some fellowship times for the coming weeks and months to review spiritual growth. During those sessions freely confess areas of difficulty as well as celebrate evidence of spiritual growth.

5. Where do you go next? The ending of a spiritual formation cycle will include times of celebration and plans for moving into

the next cycle of discipleship development. Rather than addressing all areas of need at one time, limiting cycles to one to three areas of growth will provide the opportunity for meaningful spiritual formation to take place.

Consider writing and sharing a spiritual autobiography with a few other disciples. A spiritual autobiography can help you see God's handiwork throughout your life and explore areas for spiritual growth. You may wish to use your ministry team or church small group as a place to share and discuss your spiritual autobiography.

Personal Reflection

What does the Lord's Supper mean to you? How does using the Supper as reflection differ from the Supper focused primarily on fear of unworthiness?

CONCLUSION

My home missionary parents moved our family from southern Illinois to upstate New York when we were quite young. I think nearly every aspect of our lives experienced some kind of impact from the relocation. The mountains of snow from that first winter have not melted from my mind's eye. We would soon learn to put away our toy trucks so our living room could become sacred church space. And how many nine-year-olds get to help their dad build a baptistery in their basement?

The move had another impact—the annual pilgrimage back to Illinois and Missouri to see our kinfolk. In the days of fifty-five-miles-per-hour speed limits, baloney sandwiches at rest stops, and protecting my few square feet of back seat from an encroaching brother, the trip was not always enjoyable. Yet the journey was always worth it.

The spiritual formation journey is not always a pleasant one. Seeking to become more like Christ and learning to serve Him on behalf of the world always seems to cut away some of ourselves. Little did we know our repentance, baptism, and Spirit filling would never allow us to become satisfied with our maturation process. The Teacher still has more ways to make us in His image and to send us on His mission.

We can celebrate the journey of spiritual formation as long as we remember the One who is guiding us and setting the destination. When we start fighting over square footage of back-seat vinyl or complaining about another meal at a roadside picnic table, then we know we have forgotten the reason for the journey. Fortunately, the Teacher is always with us. He will always cut away things that easily beset us. He will always shape us in His image. He will always do it with His grace.

PRAYER

Let us pray our most simple prayer.

Lord, we submit again to Your guiding hand. We will stay there until the journey is finished. Thy kingdom come, Thy will be done.

In Jesus' name,

Amen

Notes

CHAPTER 1

1. See Hebrews 5:12–6:3.

2. K. Pargament, *The Pychology of Religion and Coping: Theory, Research, Practice* (New York: Guilford Press, 1997) 32.

3. J. Carmody, "Spiritual Formation" in *Dictionary of Pastoral Care and Counseling*, ed. R. J. Hunter (Nashville, TN: Abingdon Press, 2005), 1217.

4. See II Corinthians 5:17–21.

5. I am indebted to one of my UGST students, Philip Johnson, for bringing this analysis to my attention. This application of sacred escape, however, is my own.

6. See Matthew 5:13–16.

7. See Romans 12:3–8.

8. See Joel 2:28–29; Acts 2:16–18.

CHAPTER 2

1. H. Ashby Jr., *Our Home Is Over Jordan: A Black Pastoral Theology* (St. Louis: Chalice Press, 2003).

2. For an examination of public liturgies and the impact they have on individuals and communities see J. K. A. Smith, *You Are What You Love: The Spiritual Power of Habit* (Grand Rapids, MI: Brazos Press, 2016).

3. The word *teaching* in Matthew 28:19 (KJV), is better translated "make disciples" (NKJV). Teaching in verse 20 comes from a completely different Greek word than *to make disciples* in verse 19.

4. Jesus' description of the true vine reminds us that alternatives exist. His original hearers probably thought of the nation of Israel as the true source of salvation and all good promise from Israel being in relationship with covenant God. See R. A. Culpepper, *The Gospel and Letters of John* (Nashville, TN: Abingdon Press, 1998).

5. Human efforts to satisfy religious urges may generate substitute forms of love. Jesus accused the Jews who sought to kill Him for healing on the Sabbath of not having the love of God in them (John 5:42). See L. Morris, *The Gospel according to John* (Grand Rapids, MI: Eerdmans, 1995).

CHAPTER 3

1. See II Corinthians 5:18–20.

2. See I Corinthians 4:1–4.

3. See Ephesians 2:8–9.

4. See Ephesians 5:20–21.

5. www.microsoft.com/investor/stock/stocksplit/stockcalc .aspx. The figures in this section are based on information from just prior to the time of publication.

6. www.msn.com/en-us/money/savingandinvesting/stocks -your-parents-should-have-bought-in-the-year-you-were -born/ss-bbtw5ti#image=10

7. See Luke 7:19–28.

8. www.businessinsider.com

9. See Jeremiah 29:4–7.

10. For additional detail on God's continuous redemptive plan throughout both the Old and New Testaments see M. W. Goheen, *A Light to the Nations: The Missional Church and the Biblical Story* (Grand Rapids, MI: Baker Books, 2005). Also C. J. H. Wright, *The Mission of God Unlocking the Bible's Grand Narrative* (Downers Grove, IL: InterVarsity Press, 2006).

11. See John 8:10–12.

12. See Mark 11:17.

13. See Romans 1:6; 3:1–2.

14. For a decade-by-decade review of such changes in the UPCI's global missions programs see D. Scott, *The Evolving World of Foreign Missions: The Historical Saga of a World Missions Vision by the United Pentecostal Church International* (Hazelwood, MO: UPCI General Foreign Missions Division, 2009).

15. See II Kings 15:1–7 for an example.

CHAPTER 4

1. See D. K. Bernard's *The New Birth* for the role of baptism in water and spirit for entry into the body of Christ (Hazelwood, MO: Word Aflame, 1984).

2. For a more complete examination of Pauline pastoral theology see J. W. Thompson, *Pastoral Ministry according to Paul: A Biblical Vision* (Grand Rapids, MI: Baker Books, 2006).

3. B. J. Molina and J. H. Nevrey, *Portraits of Paul: An Archaeology of Ancient Personality* (Louisville, KY: Westminster John Knox Press, 1996).

4. See I Corinthians 12:1–3.

5. For additional information on the relationship between thinking on godly things and remaking the mind see H. C. Cox, *Rewiring Your Preaching: How the Brain Processes Sermons* (Downers Grove, IL: InterVarsity Press, 2013).

6. See I Corinthians 6:20.

7. Paul's household codes included masters and servants because households in those days included business life as well as domestic life. For additional examination of this principle see D. G. Garland, *Family Ministry: A Comprehensive Guide* (Downers Grove, IL: InterVarsity Press, 2012).

8. M. Dawn, *Reaching Out without Dumbing Down: A Theology of Worship for the Turn--of-the-Century Culture* (Grand Rapids, MI: Eerdmans, 1995).

9. M. W. Goheen, *A Light to the Nations: The Missional Church and the Biblical Story* (Grand Rapids, MI: Baker, 2011).

10. See Hebrews 8:1–6.

11. See John 10.

12. This general model of a corporate worship service comes from passages such as Isaiah 6. See C. M. Cherry, *The Worship Architect: A Blueprint for Designing Culturally Relevant and Biblically Faithful Services* (Grand Rapids, MI: Baker Academic, 2010).

13. See James 4.

14. See Acts 4; 5.

15. See James 5:13–16.

16. See Acts 19:1–7.

17. For additional reading on the relationship between baptism and other elements of conversion see D. K. Bernard, *The New Birth* (Hazelwood, MO: Word Aflame Press, 1984). See also G. T. Smith, *Beginning Well: Christian Conversion and Authentic Transformation* (Downers Grove, IL: InterVarsity Press, 2001).

18. See Romans 6:1–12.

19. See Luke 22:7–10.

20. See the footwashing scenario in John 13.

CHAPTER 5

1. See Matthew 28:18–20; Luke 10:3.

2. See Matthew 7:24–27.

3. Edward Wimberly, *African American Pastoral Care: Revised Edition* (Nashville, TN: Abingdon Press, 2009).

4. Readers may benefit from consulting other books as they read the Bible. Old Testament and New Testament surveys help readers see the big picture of the Bible as well as each of the sixty-six books. One might consider reading the *Apostolic Handbook Series* published by Word Aflame Press to assist in this process. Readers may want to refer to biblical dictionaries from time to time as well.

5. Jaron Lowenstein and Joel Brentlinger, "Pray for You," *Getting Dressed in the Dark* (2010).

6. See Romans 8:15; Galatians 4:6.

7. K. Issler, *Wasting Time with God: A Christian Spirituality of Friendship with God* (Downers Grove, IL: IVP, 2006), 224.

8. For an extended examination of Paul's prayers see D. A. Carson, *Praying with Paul: A Call to Spiritual Reformation,* 2nd ed. (Grand Rapids, MI: Baker Books, 2015).

CHAPTER 6

1. See Acts 9:9; 10:30.

2. See Acts 13:2–3.

3. See. Acts 14:23.

4. A review of the arguments for or against the inclusion of fasting with prayer in I Corinthians 7:5 goes beyond the scope of this book. A vast majority of English translations do not include fasting as does the KJV. Prayer stands alone in the primary Greek version of the passage as well (*Nestle-Aland Greek New Testament, 27th ed.*).

5. See Mark 2:18–22.

6. The KJV and some other translations combine prayer and fasting in this verse as with other verses mentioned above. Many scholars believe "and fasting" came later as more and more of the church connected the two disciplines. While analysis of the issue goes beyond the scope of this book, I believe the principle of prayer and fasting certainly applies in this context.

CHAPTER 7

1. Goheen, *A Light to the Nations*, 34.

2. See I Corinthians 12.

3. https://www.washingtonpost.com/news/worldviews/wp/2016/02/09/this-remarkable-chart-shows-how-u-s-defense-spending-dwarfs-the-rest-of-the-world/?utm_term=.b0cf0603bb46

4. http://www.unhcr.org/en-us/news/latest/2016/1/568e82ff6/solutions-needed-stem-global-refugee-crisis-says-grandi.html

5. See John 14:21–24.

6. See Matthew 2:10; Luke 2:10.

7. See Luke 19:37–38.

8. I Corinthians 13:13. See also I Thessalonians 1:3; 5:8; Galatians 5:5–6; Hebrews 6:10–12; and I Peter 1:21–22.

9. See Philippians 2:16–24.

10. See I Thessalonians 2:17–20.

11. See Luke 10:1–7.

CHAPTER 8

1. *Raca* and fool seem to mean the same thing in this text. *Raca* is the Aramaic form of the word represented by fool, a translation of the word from Greek. See J. Noland, *The Gospel of Matthew: A Commentary on the Greek Text* (Grand Rapids, MI: Eerdmans Publishing, 2005), 231.

2. See Matthew 18.

3. https://www.vegan.com/guides/animal-rights-and-animal-welfare/

4. I am indebted to one of my seminary pastoral care professors, Vincent DeGregoris, for the term *carefrontation*.

5. I would be remiss to at least mention the possibility of misusing Scripture to silence those who suffer. Sadly, some conservative Christians believe weak individuals should suffer in silence and continue to endure abuse. For cases regarding domestic violence see C. C. Kroeger and N. Nason-Clark, *No Place for Abuse: Biblical and Practical Resources to Counteract Domestic Violence*, 2nd Ed. (Downers Grove, IL: InterVarsity Press, 2010). For cases of church abuse see K. Blue, *Healing Spiritual Abuse: How to Break Free from Bad Church Experiences* (Downers Grove, IL: InterVarsity Press, 1993).

6. A. B. Luter, "Repentant: New Testament" in *The Anchor Bible Dictionary*, vol. 5 (New York: Doubleday, 1992), 624–27.

7. For a more comprehensive examination of a spiritual care team see E. Wilson, S. Wilson, P. Friesen, V. Friesen, L. Paulson, & N. Paulson, *Restoring the Fallen: A Team Approach to Caring, Confronting, and Reconciling* (Downers Grove, IL: InterVarsity Press, 1997).

8. See Ephesians 6, for example.

9. See Matthew 10, for example.

CHAPTER 9

1. See Matthew 6:19–24.

2. For a greater understanding of shame and honor, see J. Georges & M. Baker, *Ministering in Honor-Shame Cultures: Biblical Foundations and Practical Essentials* (Downers Grove, IL: IVP, 2016).

3. A full examination of the theology of money and tithing goes beyond the scope of this book. The author realizes the complexities of the issue relating to the discipline of financial stewardship and encourages the reader to further study the wonder and implications of Jesus' fulfilling the Old Testament law as He brought us the law of love and the Spirit.

4. https://www.hks.harvard.edu/programs/saguaro/about-social-capital accessed 6/3/17 (site discontinued).

5. See Matthew 5:13–16.

6. See Matthew 28:18–19.

7. See Matthew 6:33.

8. Romans 12:19–21.

9. See Matthew 21:33–46.

CHAPTER 10

1. See Matthew 6:26.

2. Even evolutionary biologists today who may not even acknowledge the existence of God will follow the same example when they find a new species. They cannot resist God's example to give a name to their new classification.

3. J. A. Littles, *Theologically Conservative Parents' Construction of Parenting Practices: A Study of United Pentecostal Church Families* (Doctoral dissertation) (University of Delaware: Newark, DE, 2003).

4. A. Hochschild, *The Second Shift: Working Families and the Revolution at Home* (New York: Penguin, 2012).

5. We should not assume all people in leadership positions must work outside of the church in addition to their church responsibilities. Paul chose this option for a variety of reasons, as can be seen in his writings here in Thessalonians as well as in the

Corinthian correspondence. In fact, he affirmed the option of other leaders drawing their livelihood from the church. (See I Corinthians 9.)

6. See II Thessalonians 3:7–9.

7. See I Timothy 5 and James 1:27.

8. L. Ryken, *Redeeming the Time: A Christian Approach to Work and Leisure* (Grand Rapids, MI: Baker, 1995), 201.

9. The following primary areas of the discussion follow from Ryken's book. Ryken, *Redeeming the Time,* 197–204.

10. As Ryken points out in his book, some jobs will likely be abandoned by a new convert considering their work as a gift from God. Jobs, both legal and illegal, that harm others or oneself and that dishonor God would call one to leave that position. Some jobs would call for a change in core values to transition from harming others to serving others in the same position. For example, business practices involving deceit and defrauding others would call for a change to honesty. Cutthroat competition that forces others to lose if you are to win would call for appropriately living out the commandment to love neighbors as evidence of loving God.

11. The Sermon on the Mount contains concentrated and direct teaching on Kingdom living (Matthew 5–7). The sermon addresses all areas of life. Spending time in prayer, study, and conversation with other disciples will provide a Kingdom-centered perspective on serving God and others.

12. See Romans 12:1–3; Ephesians 6:5–8.

13. See Genesis 3:17–19.

14. N. Wirzba, *Living the Sabbath: Discovering the Rhythms of Rest and Delight* (Grand Rapids, MI: Brazos Press, 2006).

15. I would like to thank one of my Urshan College colleagues, Dr. Ann Ahrens for bringing this little book to my attention. While laboring on this book, Ann came to my office for a brief Sabbath where we discussed God's lavish love and the wonder of living out God's mission in real time . . . even when that real time has pain and laments. Our brief Sabbath brought hope, faith, and joy to both of us. See W. Brueggemann, *Sabbath as Resistance: Saying No to the Culture of Now* (Louisville, KY: Westminster John Knox Press, 2014).

16. Brueggemann, Sabbath, 87.

17. Wirzba, *Living the Sabbath*, 132.

18. See John 15 and Galatians 5:22–26.

CHAPTER 11

1. Mark 6:48. The "passing by" language recalls God passing by Moses after the golden calf crisis. Moses asked to see God's glory. God renewed His covenant name, "passed by," and displayed gracious care for His people. This gracious care provided the context for reconciliation after Israel's corporate idolatry failure.

2. While the language of "practicing the presence of God" has some connections to a seventeenth-century monk named Brother Lawrence, my primary sources for this discipline as outlined here are the biblical text and Christ who is present with us in the Spirit today.

3. See Psalm 138:6; Proverbs 3:34.

CHAPTER 12

1. See Galatians 3:1–6.

CHAPTER 13

1. https://www.techopedia.com/definition/4624/avatar

2. http://www.shiftcomm.com/blog/social-media-and -impact-theory/

3. Julie Huynh citing work of Matthias Mel https://ubrp .arizona.edu/study-finds-no-difference-in-the-amount-men -and-women-talk/

CHAPTER 14

1. Allen Verhey, "Remember, Remembrance" in *The Anchor Bible Dictionary* vol. 5 (1992), 668–69.

2. Verhey, "Remember," 668.

3. See Edward Wimberly. *African American Pastoral Care: Revised Edition* (Nashville, TN: Abingdon Press, 2008).

4. See Gordon T. Smith, *Beginning Well: Christian Conversion and Authentic Transformation* (Downers Grove, IL: IVP, 2001) for helpful guidance in writing a spiritual autobiography.